WHERE DID OUR GAME GO?

Where Did Our Game Go?

Inside College Football's Billion-Dollar Transformation

Nick Douglas

Dean Douglas

©2025 All Rights Reserved. No portion of this book may be reproduced, stored in a retrieval system, or transmitted in any form or by any means—electronic, mechanical, photocopy, recording, scanning, or other—except for brief quotations in critical reviews or articles without the prior permission of the author.

Published by Game Changer Publishing

Cover Design: Skylar Ringenbach

Paperback ISBN: 978-1-968250-17-1

Hardcover ISBN: 978-1-968250-18-8

Digital ISBN: 978-1-968250-19-5

www.GameChangerPublishing.com

DEDICATION

We would like to dedicate this book to the fans, all of you who have carried this great sport through every era. Especially to the fans of the Pac-12, who have watched more than just games, but watched a chapter of college football slowly close.

From Rose Bowl sunsets to late-night kickoffs that became part of the sport's folklore, your loyalty built something uniquely your own—a conference where history and geography combined in a way no boardroom could ever replicate.

College football was never built by television executives or contract lawyers. It was built by the people who kept showing up—in sun, in rain, in heartbreak, in hope. It was built by student sections packed before kickoff, by generations who made Saturdays into tradition, and of course, by those who tuned in to games all across the country each and every Saturday. We are all fans of the game, and the game matters because we care about it.

Today, the landscape continues to shift. Conferences fracture, rivalries dissolve, and different interests carve up the map. But the game's heartbeat never came from this. It came from you—the ones who never stopped believing that college football, at its core, was something worth investing in emotionally.

So this book is for you. For the fans who've endured the change, questioned it, and stayed with it anyway. You are, and always have been, the reason this game endures.

BEFORE WE DIVE IN

Just to say thanks for buying and reading our book,
we'd love to connect!

Scan the QR Code Here:

WHERE DID OUR GAME GO?

INSIDE COLLEGE FOOTBALL'S BILLION-DOLLAR TRANSFORMATION

NICK DOUGLAS AND DEAN DOUGLAS

AUTHOR'S NOTE

Welcome to *Where Did Our Game Go? Inside College Football's Billion-Dollar Transformation.*

Like it or not, the game is changing.

College football is the stage where America's rawest passions, traditions, and ambitions collide. To understand it is to comprehend the stories of families gathered around radios in the 1940s, listening to grainy broadcasts of bowl games; of cities like Tuscaloosa and State College swelling beyond their borders every fall Saturday; of young men who gave everything on the field then traded jerseys for uniforms during two world wars. It is a tapestry of triumph and turmoil, a reflection of a nation that loves nothing more than a fight worth having.

Yet, for all its enduring glory, college football has never had the luxury of stability. Its origins in the late 19th century were chaotic and violent—a bruising and bloody spectacle that bore little resemblance

AUTHOR'S NOTE

to the high-flying game we know today. By 1905, the crisis reached a boiling point: 19 players had died on the field that year alone. The game's very existence was threatened by calls for the government to ban it outright. It was President Theodore Roosevelt, with his fervent belief in the virtues of grit and perseverance, who stepped into the fray. His intervention not only saved the sport but transformed it, laying the groundwork for modern football and igniting the tension between tradition and change that defines the game to this day.

In the decades since, college football has proven remarkably resilient. It has weathered world wars, economic depressions, two global pandemics, and countless scandals. It has adapted, evolving from a regional curiosity into a billion-dollar juggernaut. And yet, for all its growth and reinvention, the game has never faced a predicament quite like the one it faces today.

Today, college football stands at a crossroads, shifted by forces that threaten to reshape its soul. Conference realignment has shattered some long-standing rivalries and geographical identities, with schools uprooted from their histories and thrust into leagues that promise riches but little emotional connection. The once-stable rhythm of the sport—a mix of regional pride, traditional rivalries, and measured progress—has been disrupted by the raw calculus of television markets and billion-dollar media deals. The Pac-12 conference, once a cornerstone of West Coast football, now teeters on the brink of irrelevance. Even storied rivalries like Oklahoma vs. Oklahoma State are casualties of this seismic shift.

The game itself is evolving in ways that both thrill and unsettle. Ten years of the four-team playoff led to the implementation of a 12-team playoff, which offers an exhilarating new stage for top programs to

AUTHOR'S NOTE

compete for championships. Meanwhile, the introduction of name, image, and likeness (NIL) rights has upended the sport's economic ecosystem, creating a frenzied marketplace where players negotiate sponsorships and teams vie for the biggest war chests. This newfound freedom has empowered athletes but also raised thorny questions about fairness, sustainability, and the widening chasm between haves and have-nots.

Compounding this transformation is the transfer portal, a tool that has revolutionized player mobility. What began as a means to streamline transfers has evolved into a quasi-free agency system, where players can move programs annually in pursuit of playing time, NIL deals, or championship aspirations. While this has injected fresh intrigue into roster-building, it has also eroded the sense of continuity that once defined college teams. Will these trends converge into a system where loyalty is overshadowed by opportunism, or will the sport find a way to balance freedom and tradition?

And then there is the NCAA, the biggest question mark in this whole concoction of seismic shifts. The organization's grasp on the sport it once controlled has been reduced to a tentative grip, and its future role in college football—if it has one at all—remains one of the most pressing uncertainties facing the game. We will dive into where we see them fitting in.

But if history teaches us anything, it is that college football endures. It survived the Spanish flu in 1918 and the COVID-19 pandemic a century later. It adapted to Roosevelt's reforms, embraced television's rise in the 1950s, and weathered the Supreme Court's 1984 decision that dismantled the NCAA's monopoly on broadcasting rights. At every turn, the sport has faced existential threats, and at every turn it

AUTHOR'S NOTE

has emerged, typically fielding a stronger product than previously. From the fields of the Ivy League in the 1890s to the sprawling stadiums across the country today, the game remains on an upward trajectory.

To those who tune in every Saturday for the thrill of the unexpected—to watch Appalachian State topple Michigan or to see a walk-on quarterback lead his team to victory—this book is for you. To those who feel the ache of lost rivalries and the tug of nostalgia for simpler times, this book is for you. And to those who wonder what the future holds for a game that means so much to so many, this book is for you.

If you are looking for a memoir on college football that talks about how the game we love is ending and the good ol' days are what we should return to, this is not the book for you.

Irrespective of opinion, this is for those looking to understand the dynamics that have shaped the shift across our storied sport of college football.

It's time to take a look inside college football's billion-dollar transformation and answer the question:

Where did our game go?

CONTENTS

Introduction	xv
Chapter 1	1
Chapter 2	9
Chapter 3	17
Chapter 4	23
Chapter 5	29
Chapter 6	37
Chapter 7	45
Chapter 8	53
Chapter 9	61
Chapter 10	71
Chapter 11	85
Chapter 12	93
Chapter 13	99
Chapter 14	105
Chapter 15	113
Chapter 16	117
Chapter 17	123
Conclusion	133
Afterword	137
Thank You For Reading Our Book!	141

INTRODUCTION

College football.

Those two words are more than just a phrase—they represent an embodiment of culture, a way of life, and a tradition that countless fans have embraced for over a century. If you've ever walked the campus of a football powerhouse on a crisp fall Saturday, you've felt it. Electricity is in the air as the fans begin to gather. The band triumphantly starts the fight song, and the crowd shouts the lyrics. The back and forth on the gridiron creates an emotional whirlwind for both sides. Perhaps you, the spectator, can't help but lose your voice after several third downs, with a goal-line stand as the cherry on top that has you hoarse Sunday morning.

If you've been around this game, you know the sport of college football is something sacred. The rivalries, heroes, heartbreaks, and pride of communities large and small are captured in one grand event.

INTRODUCTION

Now, however, the college football landscape has changed. Not in subtle ways but in fundamental, seismic shifts that have left even the most die-hard fans asking, "What the hell is going on?" The product within the lines on gameday is largely the same, but everything beyond the lines and into the headlines about today's sport barely resembles the college football you grew up with. A storm of change is sweeping through every corner of the game—from conference alignments to the money at play, from athletes' rights to the very essence of amateurism. The ground is shifting, and the looming question remains: when and where will things settle?

Let's take a step back and figure out how we got here.

For most of its history, college football has been relatively stable. Sure, it had its controversies, scandals, and ongoing debates, but it had a stable rhythm and structure: this group of teams plays this group of teams, these teams recruit these players, these players develop in this program, this program grows under this coach's leadership, etc.

But since the late 2010s, that rhythm has been thrown into chaos, and it hasn't happened by accident. It's been in the works for a while now, but it's finally breaching the surface. We are witnessing the culmination of a confluence of factors—politics, money, media, technology, and the rise of player empowerment.

Whether you're a diehard fan, a student, or a casual college football watcher who enjoys the entertainment on a Saturday, you're here because you're intrigued by the most celebrated sport in America—the only one that can fill a stadium with exponentially more people than the local town has the infrastructure to support. We've uncov-

INTRODUCTION

ered the truth about the inside story of **why** and **how** college football has been turned upside down and where the sport is going from here.

To dissect the forces driving the sport into this vortex, we'll explore the events that have sparked the controversies and the lawsuits that have redefined the rules. We'll expose the untold truth about the behind-the-scenes power struggles that continue to rule our game. We'll pull back the curtain on the deals that shook the foundations of college football, dissect the battles over media rights and conference supremacy, and explain how the effects of what seemed like simple decisions snowballed into the sport's most transformative era.

You might remember Texas and Oklahoma dropping the bombshell news in 2021 that they were leaving the Big 12 Conference to join the Southeastern Conference, or the SEC. On the surface, this could seem like a simple shuffling of teams. However, this would later prove to be much more of a declaration of war, sending shockwaves through every athletic department in the country. The Big 12 conference, established in 1994, was home to several national champions across all sports. Nebraska (1997), Oklahoma (2000), and Texas (2005) all hold football national championships from their days in the Big 12.

But in the summer of 2021, they sat on the brink of uncertainty. Losing two of its anchor tenants is predictably the first domino to fall in a conference headed for oblivion. Scrambling for survival, it fended off poachers while attempting to rebuild its credibility. Then, in the aftermath, a feeding frenzy began. The other Power Five conferences, which include the best teams in college football, the Big Ten, the ACC, and the Pac-12, all raced to secure their footing in a new world order in college sports. This new era was not dictated by history and

INTRODUCTION

tradition but instead by media contracts, television markets, and billion-dollar deals.

College football had long been a profitable enterprise, but in recent years, the stakes have soared to unprecedented, arguably uncontrollable heights.

So why is this happening?

How did we get here?

Where did our game go?

Where *does* our game go from here?

We're here to answer all of that and more, as we take a look inside college football's billion-dollar transformation.

CHAPTER 1

To understand why there is so much commotion around college football nowadays, you have to follow the money. Television networks, most notably ESPN and Fox Sports, have poured billions into holding the broadcasting rights of these games, commonly referred to throughout this book as "media rights" contracts. Conferences began to act not as stewards of collegiate competition but as corporate entities jockeying for prime positions in a new media ecosystem. The signing of the Big Ten's massive, seven-year, $8 billion media rights deal in 2022 was not just about televising games; it was a strategic move that cemented the conference's status as a behemoth in the sport. This set off a domino effect. The SEC, already flexing its muscle, tightened its grip on college football's narrative by forming an exclusive deal with ESPN, securing a windfall that only further widened the gap between the haves and have-nots.

The SEC, often viewed as the most competitive conference in America, had been strengthened immensely. They could sit back and watch the rest of the playing field scramble and fend for survival in real time, and they did.

But it wasn't just the conferences making moves. There was another storm brewing.

The athletes who give the game its lifeblood, began to seize control of their own destinies. The NCAA, long criticized for its stringent rules preventing players from profiting off their own names, images, and likenesses (NIL), faced mounting pressure from lawsuits and public outcry. The rules had become outdated, and cavaliers like Reggie Bush, Johnny Manziel, and Donald De La Haye were willing to face immense scrutiny and risk their eligibility for the sake of future athletes having freedoms that they did not.

De La Haye, in particular, the least popular of the three at the time, has grown in popularity among younger generations after his story was widely publicized on YouTube. De La Haye was a punter at UCF, committing to the Knights in 2015 out of high school and going winless his freshman year. In the offseason before the 2017 season, the NCAA got wind of a YouTube channel that De La Haye was using to document his life as a college football player.

The verdict from the NCAA? De la Haye had to do one of three things:

1. Delete his channel entirely.
2. Demonetize his channel, as the NCAA forbade its athletes from profiting off their athletic ability aside from their scholarships. He was also not allowed to have his likeness or name in any of his videos if he decided to continue the channel.
3. Sacrifice his career in college football, but continue to operate his channel and leverage this opportunity to call out the NCAA's dated rules.

De La Haye ultimately chose option three at the cost of his scholarship and NCAA eligibility in 2015, coming off a winless season. He gave up the opportunity to play on a team that went on the *wildest* turnaround in two years that the game has ever seen. The Knights went *undefeated* in 2017. Yes, the 0–12 Knights in 2015 turned around and went 14–0 two seasons later, including a Conference Championship and a dominant Peach Bowl victory over No.7 Auburn.

So where was De la Haye during the run? Well, he sat at home. Yet another victim of "a modern form of slavery," as he described it. "My coach makes $2 million off my name. [UCF] makes millions off my name. The NCAA makes billions per year off my name. I can't make a couple thousand bucks off myself? It's idiotic, stupid, and preposterous."

It took until the summer of 2021.

The dam finally broke.

Under pressure from multiple states passing their own Name, Image, and Likeness laws and a landmark Supreme Court decision (NCAA v. Alston), the NCAA relented and opened the door for athletes to strike endorsement deals and profit on their platforms as college athletes. Just like that, the concept of amateurism—the bedrock on which college sports had been built—was shattered.

This wasn't just a policy change; it was a cultural revolution. College athletes were no longer at the mercy of the traditional system. They were entrepreneurs with the ability to leverage their platform to build personal brands, negotiate contracts, sign deals with businesses and national brands, and really do... whatever they wanted.

Quarterbacks became celebrities, and top recruits weighed not just playing time or program prestige but also the potential financial benefit that schools might bring. The recruiting game shifted into a high-stakes marketplace, with programs vying to offer not only an opportunity to compete for a championship but also a platform for players to leverage their market potential for NIL opportunities.

THE TRANSFER PORTAL

This came about as a totally separate concept, but it didn't take long for the transfer portal to begin working in tandem with new NIL laws. It was introduced separately from all NIL discussions on October 15, 2018. This altered the traditional recruiting landscape and player movement dynamics quite a bit in the few seasons prior to NIL. Technically speaking, the transfer portal is an online database that lists student-athletes interested in changing schools. It was created as an NCAA compliance tool to streamline the transfer process, making it more efficient for both players and coaches.

Before the portal's creation, players had to seek permission to contact other schools, and coaches could restrict their options. When a player pops up in the transfer portal, schools can immediately begin recruiting them. This system effectively created a form of free agency in college football, allowing athletes to seek better opportunities or playing time at different schools without the penalty of sitting out a season.

As of 2024-2025, there are two transfer windows: December 9-28 and April 16-25. During these periods, players can enter their names in the portal, signaling their availability to other programs. However, entering the portal doesn't guarantee a transfer; players can withdraw their names and stay at their current school, though school policies vary as to how a player might return after trying their hand in the portal.

The portal's impact on college football has been significant. It has increased player mobility and forced coaches to adapt their recruiting strategies. For coaches, it has become a crucial tool for roster management. If there is a glaring hole on your roster, why not reach into the portal and fill that gap with a day-one starter? If there is a player on the national championship roster from last season, why not replace your starter with a champion? It's easy to see how the transfer portal presented new challenges and opportunities for programs adapting to this evolving system.

The portal reached new heights in early 2024 when the NCAA eliminated restrictions on the number of transfers an academically eligible athlete can make during their college career.

Previously, a player could have a one-time transfer with no penalty. Any second transfer needed a waiver approval from the NCAA. This change in 2024 opened the door for players to transfer multiple times without penalties, provided they maintain good academic standing. This created an off-season of full-on "free agency" in college football every year with no multi-year commitment on the athlete's part. The portal became this hotbed of player movement, upending team rosters and redefining championship contention in a single offseason. Coaches were forced to adapt or be left behind, turning every signing day into a frenzy of speculation and strategy. Couple this with a lack of regulation around NIL deals, and you've got something that resembles the Yankees in the late 1900s, where whoever pays the most builds the best roster.

In the midst of all this turmoil, perhaps the most important group of people beyond the players suiting up, the fans, have been left... bewildered.

The game they grew up loving morphed into something unrecognizable. Politics and power dynamics govern every aspect of the sport. Tradition? Rivalries? Conference pride? All these cherished elements seem increasingly secondary to the juggernaut of television revenue, NIL deals, and conference realignment.

The question lingers in every sports bar, tailgate, and living room that tunes in on Saturday afternoons: *What is happening to college football?*

But the story is not just about the high-profile drama. It affects everyone down to the small schools struggling to keep up, the mid-major programs caught in the crossfire of realignment, and the alumni who wonder if their school will ever have a place in the new college football hierarchy. Through the rise and fall of conferences, the formation of *Survivor*-style alliances, and the politics that come with all this, someone is bound to get the short end of the stick.

Frankly, no one is safe.

College football is in the midst of an identity crisis. For adamant followers of the sport, questions arise every day about fairness, what it means to be a student-athlete, and the role of education in an increasingly commercialized sport.

Will the game remain true to its roots, or will it become just another arm of professional entertainment dictated by the whims of television executives and corporate interests?

This book is a journey through that storm. It is a chronicle of the forces that have collided to bring us to this point, an exploration of the controversies, backroom deals, lawsuits, and power plays that have reshaped the sport. It's about the schools that have fought for their place in the sun and those left scrambling in the shadows. It's about the athletes who have seized their moment and the fans who have watched the game they love morph into something new and, at times, unsettling.

This isn't just about college football's survival. It's about its transformation. The truth is, we are all still figuring out what the game will look like year after year.

But one thing is certain: the sport is in motion, evolving right before our eyes. Buckle up because what comes next will define college football for generations to come.

This is the story of how the game is changing, why this is happening, and what it means for every player, coach, fan, and institution tied to the storied tradition of college football.

Let's take this journey together, starting with a memory we all share.

CHAPTER 2

Note: For added detail and description, parts of this chapter are written from Nick's first-person perspective.

On Friday, March 13, 2020, students across the country left for spring break. This year, however, was different. An unusual topic was rapidly gaining momentum, and anxious chatter filled campuses as everyone, including students, faculty, and even the janitors, speculated on what this new "coronavirus" might mean for the weeks ahead.

There was some chatter about how folks had come back to the U.S. from overseas and had this virus, but there was some skepticism about whether it was highly contagious, how it was transmitted, who it affected, etc. No one knew the full scale of what was coming.

My family had planned our annual ski trip like we always did, slotting it neatly into the spring break calendar. Little did we know what was in store. On the plane, there was a lot of conversation about this disease, COVID-19, from both passengers and crew. The cabin echoed with conjecture, fear, and skepticism. Some countries, like Italy, were closing their borders. The U.S. had blocked Chinese nationals from coming into the country, as China was rumored to be where it had originated. The media was in a frenzy, twisting and turning these decisions into a political issue rather than focusing on sharing the truth, irrespective of opinion.

COVID-19 rapidly became the lead topic of every podcast, news article, social media site, etc. As a student, my initial thought was, *A long spring break doesn't sound so bad.*

As our ski trip progressed, the reality of the situation began to sink in. News updates came in waves: initial deaths were reported in various states, universities suspended classes, and major events were canceled across the country. Suffice it to say that by the following weekend, the ski resorts had closed, and the country was in the process of locking down. We were all advised by medical professionals to spend the next few weeks "slowing the spread."

The flight home was a very odd trip. There were maybe ten passengers, and this was a flight at the end of a spring break between two major airport hubs. Even with the sparse crowd, all conversation was on the same topic. The vibe was eerie and unsettling, as if the world had shifted to a dark and dystopian axis. When I touched down a few hours later, the news hit: school was cancelled for the rest of the month. Two days later, we learned we wouldn't be returning at all for the semester.

WHERE DID OUR GAME GO?

College football? It was the last thing on my mind. Little did I know the pandemic wasn't just a global crisis; it would be the major catalyst for seismic shifts that would ripple across the United States and eventually alter the landscape of college football. The game was about to be reshaped in ways that no one—least of all a student on an extended spring break—could have imagined.

As the months went on, we moved from the lockdown spring to the standstill summer. This is when we saw the duality of America, as certain areas of the country tried to get back to normal. COVID-19 had become all too political: red states and rural counties fought for freedom and less government intervention, while traditional blue states and their cities leaned more into restrictions, frequently mentioning that this was "doing the right thing."

When it came time for discussions around college football, it looked exactly as you might expect: areas of the country that had been the least restrictive were ready to return to more normal fall activities, including college football, and proposed plans that looked promising. Other areas of the country embraced this idea of a "new normal" with heavy restrictions. In hindsight, some of these were misguided and unnecessary.

The challenge was that the country as a whole really did not have a plan to attack the virus. Vaccines were in the works from the early days, but as we have now learned, there was a lack of discourse regarding COVID-19. Approaches that varied from what the government suggested were either deemed misinformation or the mumblings of troglodytes.

The Northeast, Mid-Atlantic, and West Coast states were set on erring on the side of caution, keeping schools closed and suspending sports programs at the high school and college levels. Local officials made these decisions with varying levels of awareness, often including the catchphrase "an abundance of caution." The Midwest was highly restrictive in urban areas and big cities in states like Michigan, Illinois, and Minnesota, but slightly less so in more rural areas.

The Southern U.S. was by far the least restrictive. Anchored by Florida in the east and Texas in the southwest, schools were opened, and restaurants were full of patrons. After a few months, things were back to nearly normal!

Coming out of the summer, it seemed that organizations, municipalities, and states would each take their own approach to managing the restrictions. There didn't seem to be much in the way of unified leadership, and with the bureaucracy in full control over rules, it is understandable that this turned out to be a disorganized mess.

Let's walk through the COVID timeline together, as it played an integral role in how college football became what it is today.

March 2020

- **March 12, 2020,** the NCAA cancelled the remainder of spring sports activities, including football spring practice. This move further jeopardized the fall season, but we'll get to that later.

May 2020

- **May 6, 2020:** The NCAA Division I Council voted to allow football and basketball student-athletes to return to campus for voluntary workouts starting June 1, 2020, provided they followed local health guidelines. This was a great sign as the decision reflected the growing pressure to resume athletic activities despite ongoing concerns about the virus.
- **May 20, 2020:** The Pac-12 Conference, under Commissioner Larry Scott, announced that athletes could return to campus for voluntary workouts beginning June 15. This decision was seen as a cautious step in the right direction for the West Coast while prioritizing athlete safety.

June 2020

- **June 1, 2020:** College football programs began voluntary workouts under strict COVID-19 protocols. The workouts, limited in scope and intensity, were the first signs of a return to the football field, but this period underscored the challenges of maintaining safety.
- **June 17, 2020:** The NCAA mandated COVID-19 testing for all athletes who returned to campus for workouts, emphasizing the importance of monitoring and controlling the spread of the virus. However, the enforcement of these protocols varied widely among schools.

Late June 2020: COVID-19 outbreaks occurred at several major programs, including over twenty players who tested positive at Clemson, LSU, and Kansas State. These outbreaks raised alarms about the feasibility of conducting a football season, and some schools temporarily suspended workouts.

July 2020

- **July 9, 2020:** The Big Ten Conference, led by Commissioner Kevin Warren, became the first Power Five conference to announce a conference-only schedule for the 2020 season. Warren, newly appointed as commissioner, faced intense scrutiny and pressure as he navigated the unprecedented challenges posed by the pandemic. The decision was driven by the desire to maintain control over testing and protocols, limiting travel and exposure to other teams.
- **July 10, 2020:** The Pac-12, following the Big Ten's lead, announced a conference-only schedule for its fall sports, including football. Commissioner Larry Scott, known for his cautious approach, emphasized the need to prioritize the health and safety of student-athletes, even as doubts about the season's viability grew.
- **July 13, 2020:** The NCAA released updated "Resocialization of Collegiate Sport" standards, which included strict guidelines for regular testing, hygiene practices, and quarantine protocols. These guidelines were intended to standardize safety measures, but enforcement remained inconsistent across conferences.

- **July 20, 2020:** The SEC, under Commissioner Greg Sankey, delayed the start of football practices until August 17 and prohibited full-contact practices until further notice. Sankey, known for his calculated yet aggressive approach, continued to express optimism about the season while acknowledging the evolving nature of the pandemic.
- **July 28, 2020:** The NCAA announced that student-athletes who opted out of a season due to COVID-19 would retain their scholarships, providing reassurance to those worried about the risks of playing during a pandemic.

August 2020

- **August 5, 2020:** UConn became the first FBS program to cancel its football season due to COVID-19, citing not just safety concerns but that "ultimately, the student-athletes would rather have preserved their year of eligibility" and focused on "competing under more typical circumstances during the 2021 season."

This was an interesting point of emphasis, as the NCAA had not yet issued any verdict on whether playing in a COVID-19 season would impact an athlete's eligibility. They had determined that *scholarships* were unaffected, but there was no verdict on whether one of the four years an athlete has *eligibility* was affected. This issue clearly came across the NCAA's desk shortly after this announcement, and they would reach their decision over the next few weeks.

Chaos reigned as the commissioners and the NCAA tried to address juxtaposition that was athlete health and safety and a desire to have football in the fall of 2020. Certain conference executives wanted it to work, and athletes would soon weigh in on whether playing this season was important.

Would the health risks and politics regarding COVID-19 derail the desire to compete on the gridiron that fall, or would athletes surge past all the minutiae surrounding this virus and unite around one of the most unifying pieces of our society: sports?

CHAPTER 3

Show-stopping news came at the beginning of what was projected to be a dark week for college football.

On the morning of August 10, 2020, citing the "uncertainty at this point in time in our country," the Big Ten, under Commissioner Kevin Warren, announced the formal cancellation of the entire 2020 football season. Warren had just revealed plans a month earlier for an all-conference schedule, but clearly, he had a change of heart.

"As time progressed," Warren stated, "and after hours of discussion with our Big Ten Task Force for Emerging Infectious Diseases and the Big Ten Sports Medicine Committee, it became abundantly clear that there was too much uncertainty regarding potential medical risks to allow our student-athletes to compete this fall."

The Big Ten announcement looked to be the first big domino falling in what was going to be a wipeout of events. In the summer of 2020, there were waves of virtue-signaling efforts to "play it safe" when, in reality, the science did not support that these players were more at risk playing football than they were at doing a multitude of daily activities. "We just need to constantly do the right thing from a medical standpoint to make sure our student-athletes are in an environment that remains both healthy and safe," Warren claimed.

One day later, Pac-12 Commissioner Larry Scott followed suit and canceled the 2020 football season for *his* conference.

Traveling to the Southeast and East Coast, the ACC made a point to embrace Cameron Wolfe, an infectious disease expert at Duke University. In an interview with *Sports Business Daily*, he spoke about the virus's impact on these athletes and how doctors had learned enough about the virus in the last several months to approve a risk-mitigated fall season, directly contradicting Warren's and Scott's moves.

Columns firing back at Warren came in waves as most of the country publicly criticized him for the move. Radio personalities came up with aggressive examples with comments like, "College football players have a higher chance of dying while driving to practice than they do contracting the virus while playing football." Given that car accidents kill over 20,000 people per year (NHTSA), this statistic would be correct.

It wasn't just the sports pundits; it was also the players. Throughout history, athletes have threatened to boycott their sports, but this was one of the few examples of an inverse boycott. The hashtag #WeWantToPlay trended on social media, led by star players like Ohio State's Justin Fields. Fields launched a petition that garnered hundreds of thousands of signatures in a matter of days.

Fields asked for three things:

1. The Big Ten Conference immediately reinstate the 2020 football season.
2. The Big Ten players/teams be granted the right to make their own choice on whether they wish to play.
3. The Big Ten allows players to opt out without penalty or repercussion.

At this point, the college football world was in an uproar, and a lot of activity would stem from this announcement, so...

Back to the timeline.

August 2020 continued

- **August 12, 2020**: In light of the Big Ten announcement, the NCAA Division I Board of Directors approves a blanket eligibility waiver for all fall athletes, ensuring that they do **not** lose a year of eligibility regardless of whether they compete in the fall or spring. This decision provides some relief to athletes facing uncertainty about their future.
- **August 19, 2020**: The ACC, SEC, and Big 12, under the leadership of Commissioners John Swofford, Greg Sankey, and Bob Bowlsby, respectively, reaffirm their commitment to playing a fall football season. These conferences, representing the heart of college football's most passionate regions, push forward with modified schedules with the argument that a season can be safely conducted.

Greg Sankey, in particular, emerged as a leading advocate for playing, emphasizing the need to adapt to the new reality while ensuring the safety of players. With this move, the approach taken by Kevin Warren and Larry Scott appeared more aligned with political winds than with a sincere desire to protect student-athletes. In fact, while the SEC allowed limited-capacity attendance throughout the season, Kevin Warren planned to travel south to sit in the crowd at SEC games, even as his own conference remained sidelined all season.

Wait, what?

Yes, you read that right. Mississippi State University allowed for reduced capacity in Davis Wade Stadium in Starkville. This meant player families would be allowed to attend, and this list of player families would include Kevin Warren. Professionally, he was known as the commissioner of the Big Ten conference. Outside of work, he was the father of Mississippi State tight end Powers Warren.

Though Kevin Warren was determined to hold his ground and keep Big Ten athletes from competing, he was prepared to travel several hundred miles to support another college football conference. The thousands of athletes in *his* conference, which *he* was in charge of, were left to hang in the balance.

Back to our timeline

- **August 21, 2020**: Under immense public scrutiny, the Big Ten and Pac-12 face mounting pressure to reconsider their postponements of the fall football season. Parents of Big Ten players organize protests outside conference headquarters and political figures, all the way from local leaders to the president, make clear their support of a college football season. Despite the backlash, Warren and Scott stood by their decisions, citing the need for more information about COVID-19's impact on athletes.

- **Late August 2020**: As the ACC, SEC, and Big 12 finalized their schedules, they introduced their framework for the 2020 season. Reduced games, enhanced testing protocols, and the elimination of non-conference matchups (with few exceptions). Schools like Notre Dame joined the ACC for the season to ensure they'd have a full schedule, further showcasing the efforts made by some to improvise while others looked to sabotage.

CHAPTER 4

The inconsistent nature of whether to allow college football teams to play was remarkable. There was no reason to suspend or modify the season for any of these teams. Instead of defaulting to why we should cancel the season, the approach should have been, "Let's find a way to have the season go on with some restrictions."

Let's look at the approach taken in 1918 and 1919, when the country was in the thick of the Spanish flu epidemic. While 18 schools did not play college football in 1918, this was as much a result of student-athletes fighting in WWI as it was of the epidemic.

In fact, Woodrow Wilson believed that football was good for the morale of the country. As a result, he had various military posts around the country organize football teams, which then played against established college teams. Woodrow Wilson wrote in a letter, "It would be difficult to overestimate the value of the football experience as part of the soldier's training."[1]

This was at a time when 675,000 were killed in the U.S. by the virus.

Having personally attended football games in the fall of 2020, it was a luxury to watch football again. Amidst all the chaos, an election on the horizon, confusion, depression, and everything in between, the SEC granted fans an all-conference schedule.

Week in and week out, teams were forced to prepare for a noteworthy opponent. No non-conference filler opponents. No paying a lesser opponent several million dollars to travel and get blown out in front of a halfway-filled home crowd. Every game became important.

But let's be clear: by the fall of 2020, the world had been turned upside down. Irrespective of conference lines or state borders, football was not immune to the tidal wave of disruption caused by the COVID-19 pandemic. In a time defined by isolation, uncertainty, and loss, college football players—arguably the heart of many campus communities—stood together in an unexpected show of unity. **They wanted to play no matter the cost**. No matter the hurdles.

It wasn't just about the game; it was about having the opportunity to identify with their communities. For the same reason doctors love going to hospitals and lawyers love being in the courtroom, these athletes loved taking the field alongside their brothers, primed for battle. As their game was taken away from them, they rallied time and time again. Some of the most prominent players took to social media,

---

1. Wilson, Woodrow. *The Papers of Woodrow Wilson*, edited by Arthur S. Link. Princeton: Princeton University Press, 1966–1994

held press conferences, and issued heartfelt pleas. They simply wanted to be allowed to do what they loved. However, this was still left up to the conferences.

The NCAA, faced with unprecedented pressure, made a decision that was as monumental as it was temporary—or so it seemed. In an effort to adapt to the chaos, they allowed players to transfer schools without the usual one-year waiting period—a decision framed as a one-time exception. In an era of emergency measures, it was seen as a necessary adaptation. However, like many emergency measures, what was designed as a fleeting exception soon took root and established a precedent that would ripple far beyond the pandemic.

This decision was the spark that ignited the transfer portal as we know it today. Though the portal was launched in October 2018, it wasn't until COVID-19 reshaped the world that its potential truly became realized and eventually exploited. What was once a bureaucratic tool designed to help players find new homes in unique circumstances soon morphed into a mechanism that would forever alter the recruiting landscape.

Before the portal, transfers were rare and often carried a stigma—players had to sit out for a year, and the move typically signaled instability or discontent. The core of a college football team was built on recruiting high school athletes who would rise through the ranks over several seasons. Transfers from junior colleges or other universities were infrequent, seen as a supplementary addition to the foundation of young, raw talent.

But post-2020, that structure began to crumble. The transfer portal turned the once-cautious world of collegiate recruitment on its head.

No longer were high school seniors the primary target of college football coaches. Instead, experienced players who had already been battle-tested at the highest level began flooding into the portal. For some, it was a chance to find a better fit. For others, it was a strategic move to raise their profile and align themselves with new programs. Teams that once relied on cultivating talent over time were now piecing together rosters from a marketplace of athletes looking for greener pastures.

The result? A seismic shift in how championship teams were built. By the mid-2020s, it became clear that most championship rosters were shaped not by promising freshmen, but instead by seasoned veterans. Where did these veterans come from? You guessed it. Through the portal, seeking a new opportunity. The value of high school recruiting began to diminish. Why invest years into developing a young player who could leave when the portal could deliver immediate and experienced talent with a proven track record? The culture of college football was being rewritten before our eyes.

However, the transfer portal was only one part of the equation. As the dust settled on the pandemic, another storm was brewing—this time in the courtroom.

For decades, the NCAA had held a firm grip on the amateur status of its athletes, forbidding them from receiving compensation beyond their scholarships. But in 2021, that grip was finally pried loose. The Supreme Court's decision in *NCAA v. Alston* paved the way for athletes to be compensated for their name, image, and likeness (NIL). The ruling sent shockwaves through college sports, fundamentally altering the balance of power between players and institutions.

With the NIL decision, players now had the freedom to monetize their fame. What followed was a rapid escalation of deals and endorsements as athletes—particularly football players—were courted by local businesses, national brands, and notably, alumni-driven collectives. Boosters, who had long operated in the shadows of college football, now had a legitimate way to funnel money to athletes: leveraging NIL deals as the vehicle. The result was a new era of bidding wars and financial incentives, with players now making decisions not just based on the prestige of a program or its coaching staff, but on the size of the paycheck waiting for them.

The combination of the transfer portal and NIL created an almighty storm. This was the dawn of a new era in which college football began to resemble the professional leagues more than ever before. Players were no longer locked into anything; they had the flexibility to shop around for the best opportunities on and off the field and secure financial compensation in ways unimaginable just a few years earlier.

For the NCAA, the stakes had never been higher. What began as a series of emergency measures during a global pandemic had evolved into a lasting transformation of the sport. The lines between amateurism and professionalism had blurred to the point where they were nearly irrelevant. College football, once grounded in tradition and loyalty, had become a marketplace—one where money, mobility, and marketing ruled the day.

And the question remained: what's next?

As we turn the page to the next chapter of college football's evolution, it's impossible to ignore the foundational shifts that brought us to this point. The COVID-19 pandemic may have been the catalyst, but the forces that have reshaped the sport come from within the game's history.

College football's journey from tradition to transformation is far from over. In fact, it's just heating up. In the years ahead, we will see more dramatic changes as players continue to assert their power, bureaucracies and universities do their best to navigate the complexities of this new landscape, and the NCAA grapples with its fading control.

But first, we must understand how we got here, this time in a different light.

In early 2020, college football wrestled with whether to play the season that fall. A hundred years before, however, an event of different stature struck our beloved sport, but it had a similar paralyzing effect.

CHAPTER 5

Football in the early 20th century was a far cry from the spectacle we know today. We're not talking about recruitment rankings, publicity efforts, or NFL draft powerhouses. Instead, we're talking about the physical game *inside* the white lines. It was dangerous, chaotic, and often brutal. The game, much like early air travel, was a risky endeavor—its participants were at the mercy of loose rules and a lack of proper safety equipment. The forward pass, a revolutionary concept introduced in 1906, was still in its infancy, while helmets were little more than thin leather caps offering scant protection. And the death toll, a grim reminder of the sport's volatility, soon became concerning.

By 1905, the dangers of college football finally reached a tipping point. Nineteen young men lost their lives that year alone, casualties of a game played with abandon and without oversight. The carnage was so severe that it drew the attention of President Theodore Roosevelt. President Roosevelt met with representatives from various college football powerhouses and demanded reforms. The game would survive, but not without fundamental changes. Changes that would lay the groundwork for the modern sport.

As the crowds at college football games grew, so too did the influence of the game on American culture. What started as a niche pastime had, by the early 20th century, captured the imaginations of students and alumni alike. However, the road ahead was still fraught with challenges, and the survival of college football was far from guaranteed. The game was growing, but so was the movement to ban it. In 1905, the *San Francisco Call* listed off the year's fatalities: "Body blows producing internal injuries were responsible for four deaths, concussions of the brain claimed six victims, injuries to the spine resulted fatally in three cases, blood poisoning carried off two gridiron warriors, and other injuries caused four deaths."

But as we'll see, the resilience of the sport, much like its players, would endure by the relentless pursuit of greatness. In the same way, the future of college football today remains uncertain. We know it will be around, but how will it continue to evolve? Are we looking at a semi-professional league where money and mobility dictate the outcomes, or will there be a reckoning, a return to something closer to its roots?

As we mentioned, the sport looks different today than it did a century ago. Yes, facilities, recruiting, and infrastructure get exponentially more attention now than they ever did back then. On the field, talent has gotten much better, and players are stronger and more athletic, but the real difference is in what is allowed. One observer in the Yale-Harvard game in 1902 recalled seeing "a Yale man throttle—literally throttle—[a Harvard player] so that he dropped the ball."[1] Fan favorite plays of today, like the "Hail Mary" (all receivers run straight down the field), were illegal at the time, as was the "flea flicker" (popularized trick play). This era had the "flying wedge," where the ship (offense) would part the seas, and every player, in unison, would attack and trample the defense.

This is how the play was drawn up:

Bottom View (Pre-Snap Alignment):

LG　C　RG
LT　QB　RT
LH　FB　RH
LE　　RE

---

1. Watterson, John Sayle. *College Football: History, Spectacle, Controversy.* Baltimore: Johns Hopkins University Press, 2000.

- **RE = Right End**
- **RT = Right Tackle**
- **RG = Right Guard**
- **C = Center**
- **LG = Left Guard**
- **LT = Left Tackle**
- **LE = Left End**
- **QB = Quarterback**
- **LH = Left Halfback**
- **RH = Right Halfback**
- **FB = Fullback**

It is not very often that a U.S. president intervenes with American football outside of a major global threat or the national championship team going to the White House to celebrate their national championship victory. President Teddy Roosevelt was much more hands-on in his tenure. As an athlete himself, he recognized the benefits of football and saw the scrutiny that the game was under. He decided to call another meeting with the figureheads of the sport. Together, they set about making several rule changes to improve safety for college athletes, one of them establishing a regulatory body to ensure that football was monitored on an ongoing basis. Ironically, the National Collegiate Athletic Association, or NCAA, was built with this kind of foundation to create the proper landscape for football to be a safe sport. The NCAA has evolved quite a bit beyond its initial charter. We'll dive into that later in this story.

Following Roosevelt's meeting with football's figureheads, nineteen rules emerged that allowed and encouraged new styles. A "first down" was now ten yards instead of five, making plays like the flying wedge discouraged. There was a neutral zone between the lines of scrimmage. Several players were required to be "linemen," where they started and ended play on the line of scrimmage.

Other developments contributed to a much more exciting and safer sport. As discussed earlier, the forward pass was developed in 1906 and completely redefined how the game was played. The first forward pass ever thrown resulted in an incompletion and a turnover on downs—not a promising start for what turned out to be a revolutionary concept that changed the pace of football forever. Saint Louis University quarterback Bradbury Robinson threw the ball on September 5, 1906, and he connected with receiver Jack Schneider for a 20-yard touchdown later in the game. The rule change was part of a three-year effort by John W. Heisman—yes, that Heisman—who lobbied relentlessly to make the game less brutal and more appealing to spectators and players alike.

Suddenly, teams that implemented the forward pass began to rack up lopsided victories, causing a chain reaction of acceptance in the early 1900s. It also contributed to a drastically overhauled structure of the game. Defenses were now assembled to defend against the threat of the pass. This favored the offense, as passing strategy allowed for sophisticated offensive schemes. It also made the game much safer with the crush of bodies at the line of scrimmage being left to the offensive and defensive lines. Pass-catching positions became more skilled and specialized.

The game continued to develop under these rules and became much more civilized and stable. First and foremost, there were fewer deaths.

When the death rate drops in anything, things are trending in the right direction. Rosters had players emerging as stars and superstars, and there was now an NFL league to feed them into at the season's end. However, unlike most sports, when the football season concluded, that was sort of... it. There were no official rankings (yet). The season was over, and life went on... until everyone realized how uncompetitive (and un-American) this was.

We're talking about *American* football, a perpetual motion of flying bodies at all times. Life was on the line every play. The field was sacred ground for physical attacks that were illegal pretty much anywhere else. There *had* to be some way to crown a champion. However, there was no official "college football championship game," and there wouldn't be for decades. You see, the further back you go into NCAA history, the messier the crowning of national champions becomes. Case in point, the pre-BCS era featured ten split national championships. In the "old days," as longtime college football fans affectionately call it, there was never a traditional championship game that decided once and for all which team reigned supreme during that particular season. It's important to remember that until 1968, there were only four bowl games (Rose, Cotton, Orange, and Sugar), and being selected to participate in one was a huge deal. Every now and then, college football fans would be treated to a Rose or Orange Bowl game between the number one and two teams, but that was pure coincidence. Winning one of these four gave programs the opportunity to be selected as the national champion via polling.

As college football and metrics evolved, "Who was the best team?" became a yearly debate. The metrics for talent and the contributions of star athletes also became a subject of discussion among fans and analysts alike. Unlike any other sport, football uniquely illustrates the paradox that even the most exceptional talents can be rendered powerless without a great team around them. American football has more examples than any other sport of legendary players who never tasted the glory of championship victories due to the inadequacies of their teams. This harsh reality underscores football's essence as the ultimate team sport, where the collective effort often overshadows individual brilliance.

However, the sport grew in stature, and so did the recognition of extraordinary individual performances. The accolades, particularly the Heisman Trophy, became not just symbols of excellence but crucial milestones in a player's journey to the professional ranks. These honors began to serve as the ultimate sign that a player was ready for the pros, enhancing their résumé and solidifying their status before they even stepped onto an NFL field.

The Heisman Trophy recognizes the most outstanding player in college football. Its significance was best exemplified by its inaugural recipient, Jay Berwanger, who was promptly drafted as the first overall pick in the National Football League draft that spring. This marked a turning point in the game's history and can be seen as the first example where individual prowess in college football could catapult a player to the top of the sport. Perhaps this era was the peak of buying into being a part of something bigger than oneself and building something greater than what it was when you found it. The impact of an individual could now be recognized.

President John F. Kennedy's inauguration speech was received with roaring enthusiasm, where he famously said, "Ask not what your country can do for you—ask what you can do for your country." Fast forward to the modern era, and college football directly contradicts the words President Kennedy stood behind. Now, we see an increasing emphasis on what a program can do for its players on a short-term basis.

Is this better or worse for the game? For society?

You be the judge.

CHAPTER 6

College football had found its rhythm. After starting out as a brutal free-for-all, the game had begun to resemble the one we gather to watch every Saturday. Entering the 1940s, however, the world was about to change in ways that no one could have imagined, not from a pandemic standpoint but something more. Sandwiched between the Spanish flu and COVID was not a virus but a more brutal, cataclysmic event.

The gridiron had become the sacred stage for young men to prove their place in this world. Strength, strategy, and sheer willpower blended beautifully to determine the best team on a given day, forging the legends of the gridiron in that era. Just as the sport had evolved from a deadly pastime into an organized spectacle, the world was carrying out that operation inversely, transitioning from a civilized, prosperous era to a brutal, deathly era.

Enter the 1940s, a decade that would see the game (and society) stretched to its limits. World War II was the existential crisis of college football. This conflict would call upon the very young men who routinely roared with pride in the largest stadiums in the United States and force them to exchange their leather helmets for steel ones and their cleats for combat boots. The battlefield would become their new arena, and the stakes were no longer about touchdowns or titles but about life and death.

As the military draft swept across the nation, college football teams found themselves gutted. Rosters were drained of talent that had once electrified crowds and brought glory to campuses. Coaches who were once hired to strategize week after week on the gridiron were now left to strategize how to keep their programs alive. Once again, the future of college football hung in the balance.

It's rare to see a sport grow and captivate an entire nation the way American football has, then also see that same sport threatened so many times.

After a wildfire decimates a biome, new opportunities are created in the biome's rebirth. College football would do the same. Just as it has in the face of every challenge, college football finds a way to survive, adapt, and put itself back on the fast track to becoming America's most popular sport.

College football stands as a towering symbol of American exceptionalism, so deeply ingrained in the fabric of the nation that explaining it to foreigners is nearly impossible. It's more than just a game; it transcends the bounds of competition and has become a unifying force for millions. The allure of college football lies not only in its intensity but also in its passion. How it transforms otherwise quiet, unassuming towns into the premier spot where "you just had to be there."

"Growing up in Seattle, I can tell you that my best football memories are in Oxford, Mississippi, and Knoxville, Tennessee. I've got to be the first member in my bloodline that can say that," said George Davlantes, a native Washingtonian now attending school in Nashville, Tennessee. Kids like George exist across the country as enrollment booms in certain schools, largely due to the appeal of their sports teams.

The epicenter of college football glory lies in Tuscaloosa, Alabama—a city of around 100,000 residents, where the University of Alabama's Bryant-Denny Stadium boasts a seating capacity greater than that. A stadium the size of the town? Yes, and this is just one of many testaments to the sheer magnitude of college football's draw. On game days, fans and media flood in from all over the country to witness the Alabama Crimson Tide in action. The stadium, a modern-day coliseum, dwarfs the city it calls home. Thousands travel from near and far to celebrate the game taking place, even though only 100,077 fans can get a seat inside the stadium.

This phenomenon isn't unique to just one specific area of the country, as Beaver Stadium in State College, Pennsylvania, holds over 106,000 fans—more than twice the population of the town itself. On fall Saturdays, the serene Pennsylvanian countryside morphs into a sea of blue and white, with tailgates stretching for miles and the roar of the crowd echoing through the hills.

College football's traditions are unlike any other sport in the world, steeped in history and local culture. Some would argue that Baton

Rouge, Louisiana, has become more synonymous with the capital of LSU football than it has with the capital of the state of Louisiana. LSU fans have created one of **the** best atmospheres in all of sports, so electric that it has registered on the Richter scale. The ritual of fans flooding the streets, the pageantry of the marching bands, and the sheer volume of 100,000 voices create an experience that's unmatched.

Then there's Ann Arbor, Michigan, where the University of Michigan's stadium consistently draws over 107,000 fans, making it the largest stadium in the United States. The traditions at "The Big House" run deep, from the band playing "The Victors" to the iconic winged helmets of the Wolverines. These are the core elements that create a sense of continuity that links generations of fans.

College football is woven into the fabric of these towns and universities. The traditions, rivalries, and shared experiences of generations of fans—these elements combine to make college football more than just a sport. It's a living, breathing monster capable of doubling the population of small towns on game days. Where stadiums rise as monuments to the sport's grandeur, and where the passion of the fans is unrivaled in its intensity. In these towns, on these campuses, college football is more than just a pastime—it's the heartbeat of the community.

By the time World War II ended, football had become a cornerstone of American identity. The soldiers who returned home brought back a renewed sense of purpose forged on the battlefields. As they traded their uniforms back for letterman jackets and helmets, they carried with them a hunger for competition and the camaraderie they had known in the trenches. They also carried with them the GI Bill, which opened up the opportunity for a vast group of returning veterans to attend college.

At the heart of this post-war resurgence, universities across America saw their enrollments surge. With that, the talent pool for football teams was now the best it had ever been. In 1949, the two-platoon system was introduced, allowing unlimited substitution and expanded roster sizes. Players could now specialize in their positions, and coaches got much savvier in the construction of their rosters and game plans. No longer were athletes required to play both offense and defense; now, they could focus on mastering a single aspect of the game. This boosted the talent level inside the white every Saturday to the point where athletic scholarships, after years of efforts from conferences, were permitted in 1950.

The game was on fire. Young men were drawn to the idea of receiving higher education and lured by the promise of glory on the gridiron. This era saw the game evolve rapidly, as there was finally a long-standing structure and stability. Conferences became all the more important as football became the primary revenue source for most of these schools. It became much more critical to have competitive games, but also with opponents that your fans wanted to watch. Conferences provided the governing body to ensure rivalry, tradition, and regional pride. They laid out the framework for regular-season play, ensuring that teams of similar stature and geographical proximity faced each other regularly.

When teams are concerned with fending for themselves and getting greedy, it can come at the expense of a conference's existence. One of the largest scandals in our beloved game's history was the fall of a west coast football conference, a move that carried so much controversy at the time that it dominated the storylines.

We're talking about the first time this happened, in 1959.

Established in 1915, the PCC (Pacific Coast Conference) was the predecessor of what would eventually become one of the most storied conferences in college football history, until West Coast football came under siege *again* in 2023.

The "pay-for-play" practice, a staple of the game's recruiting landscape, only becomes a scandal if you're stupid enough to get caught by the NCAA, as this was a blatant violation of NCAA regulations. The University of Washington, UCLA, USC, and California were caught up in these scandals, and the commissioner of the PCC was fired. As the situation became more and more unstable, in 1959, the PCC officially disbanded, leaving a void in the college football landscape across the Western United States.

In the aftermath of the PCC's dissolution, the Athletic Association of Western Universities (AAWU) was formed, initially consisting of just five schools: California, Stanford, USC, UCLA, and Washington. These schools sought to distance themselves from their scandalous past and restore credibility to West Coast college football. However, the transition was not without its challenges, as the AAWU struggled to regain the prestige and stability that the PCC had once enjoyed.

The turning point came in 1964 when the teams of AAWU found themselves out of the "penalty box," so to speak, and expanded to include Oregon, Oregon State, and Washington State, officially becoming the Pacific-8 Conference and adopting the moniker Pac-8. This reformation marked the beginning of a new era, one where the

Pac-8 would grow to become a powerhouse conference, eventually expanding to include ten schools and later 12 (and then two for the 2024 athletic year)

However, for 60 years, the Pac-8 laid the framework for decades of fierce competition, strong matchups, and legendary moments that would define West Coast football as an integral piece of the college football landscape.

CHAPTER 7

Beyond the grand theater of college football, where history and tradition are at the core of the game's appeal, one truth reigns supreme. It's not a revelation, and it's not restricted to just football.

The '40s, '50s, and '60s saw an uncomplicated power structure in college football. The NCAA was much less overbearing than it would become in later decades and primarily served as a regulator for fair play and player safety. For as much as fans and media refer to the modern NIL and transfer portal era as the "Wild West," this era was just as wild.

There were numerous cheating scandals, mostly stemming from paying players. Just about every prominent team had a violation during this era, and rivals often turned each other in to get a competitive edge (they were all doing it). One of the most puzzling features of this era is the fact that the final AP poll was conducted before the postseason bowl games were played, which led to some very questionable national championship claims. In 1960, sixth-ranked Washington played number one, Minnesota, in the Rose Bowl, defeating the Golden Gophers 17–7. Minnesota still clung to its number one ranking due to the timing of the poll, and a bevy of other programs claimed themselves to be national champions, including Ole Miss, Missouri, and, obviously, Washington in 1960.

Speaking of Washington, they were responsible for one of the more prominent player-payment scandals of the era. Running back and return specialist Hugh McElhenny was an AP First-Team All-American for the Huskies and wound up getting drafted ninth overall by the San Francisco 49ers. According to the Pro Football Hall of Fame, "Hugh McElhenny was to pro football in the 1950s and early 1960s what Elvis Presley was to rock and roll." It sounds like a dream, but in 2004, McElhenny finally confirmed what had been speculated for decades: he had essentially taken a pay cut when he left the university to play in the NFL.

As one head coach we spoke to put it, "You can build great relationships with potential employees, but if you don't have the money to pay them, they aren't going to come work for you." He followed with, "That's the essence of recruiting in college football. You better find a way to compete in recruiting."

People will go where the money is, whether on salary or under the table, whether athlete or employee, whether greedy or conservative. Money plays a tremendous role in the way the college football system churns out players, games, matchups, etc.

College football was on the cusp of yet another seismic shift. After dealing with a ban due to violence in the game, adopting the forward pass, surviving the Spanish flu, and forming major conferences, the game was now preparing for its next quantum leap.

In 1940, college enrollment was approximately 1.5 million students. An estimated six percent of Americans had college degrees at that time. By 1950, this number had skyrocketed to around 20 percent, with nationwide enrollment booming to 2.7 million. The NCAA knew this exponentially greater alumni base was concerned with how their alma mater performed. With television emerging as a powerful new medium in the early 1950s, the NCAA quickly realized that it had the power to revolutionize college football. In 1951, the NCAA made a landmark decision to centralize control of all television rights to college football games. This move effectively cemented the NCAA's power over the broadcasting of the sport, allowing it to dictate which games would be televised and under what conditions. The decision eliminated the possibility of media egos and politics entering play and neutralized schools were beginning to strike their own television deals.

By taking control of television rights, the NCAA aimed to ensure that the profits from broadcasting were equitably distributed among its member institutions, preventing any single school from monopolizing the financial benefits.

The immediate ramifications of this decision were significant. For one, the NCAA limited the number of televised games for the sake of protecting in-person attendance. Only one national game was broadcast each week. This control allowed the NCAA to maintain a balance between generating new revenue from television and preserving the revenue streams from ticket sales. As a result, college football began to reach a much wider audience. Television brought the excitement of the sport into living rooms across America, further transforming it into the national spectacle that it was already becoming. This was yet another moment where college football appealed to the masses. This time, it was no longer reserved for those who could attend games in person.

The NCAA's strategic gamble paid off, and the decision to harness television marked the beginning of the broadcast era in college athletics. This would lay the foundation for what would eventually become a multi-billion-dollar industry, forever changing the landscape of college football and elevating it to new heights.

However, beneath this veneer of triumph, storm clouds were already gathering, hinting at the battles to come. Just as college football seemed to have reached an era of balance and prosperity, the forces that would disrupt it were quietly gaining strength, setting the stage for a future filled with upheaval and uncertainty.

A pivotal moment in 1984 forever altered the media landscape of college football. It was the dawn of an era where "media rights" would become the root of the structural changes that would affect college football. Television would come to dominate the sport. It all happened with a Supreme Court ruling that fundamentally shifted control of college football broadcasts. Before this decision, the NCAA held a tight grip on all television rights. They dictated everything.

Enter *NCAA v. Board of Regents of the University of Oklahoma*. Initiated by the University of Oklahoma and the University of Georgia, this case challenged the NCAA's monopoly over television rights, arguing that this control violated antitrust laws by restricting competition. The Supreme Court agreed, ruling in favor of the universities.

This ruling handed the reins to the conferences and, by extension, television networks that broadcast games. Just as players follow the money to play for certain programs, conferences follow the money when it comes to media networks. The typical college football fan wouldn't fret over these issues; who cares if my game is on CBS, ESPN, or Fox? That's not relevant to most fans; we get that. But the old phrase, "Money talks," rings true and will never die out. Consider it amplified here. What does this mean? Whatever those networks say... goes.

From this moment on, the media had a powerful say in how college football was presented to the public, arguably more than the NCAA. These large corporations set the stage for television contracts to become the driving force behind decision-making, conference realignments, and even the survival of entire programs.

Fast forward to today, and the 1984 ruling has paved the way for the modern landscape of media rights deals, which have since become the financial backbone of college athletics. Conferences began negotiating lucrative contracts with networks, securing billions of dollars in revenue. These deals have transformed college football into an industry where television revenue dictates the scheduling, expansion, and strategic decisions of the sport.

These massive contracts highlight the central role that television networks now play in college football. According to Bleacher Report, the SEC has a ten-year deal with ESPN that will bring around $740 million per year beginning in 2024,[1] a contract worth more than five times the value of its previous deal with CBS. Meanwhile, the Big Ten secured a seven-year, $8 billion media deal with CBS, NBC, and Fox in 2022, allowing these networks to broadcast games starting in 2023.[2] These massive contracts highlight the central role that television networks now play in college football.

The 1984 Supreme Court ruling didn't just change who controlled college football broadcasts; it marked the moment when the media became an integral player in the sport. The networks, once merely a broadcasting medium, now had the power to shape the very structure of college football. They didn't dictate any of what happens on the field, but pulled nearly every string in the evolution of the sport off the field. Today, the impact of that decision is evident. Unless something drastically alters how games are broadcast, the desires of these massive media corporations will be expressed through every multi-billion-dollar media rights contract that conferences negotiate. These dollar amounts will always remain large enough to lay the grounds for survival.

---

1. Bleacher Report. "Report: Big Ten, SEC to Hold Historic Meeting; Will Talk CFP Bracket Format, More." https://bleacherreport.com/articles/10136900-report-big-ten-sec-to-hold-historic-meeting-will-talk-cfp-bracket-format-more.
2. Bleacher Report. "Big Ten Agrees to Historic Media Rights Contract Reportedly Worth at Least $7B." https://bleacherreport.com/articles/10045812-big-ten-agrees-to-historic-media-rights-contract-reportedly-worth-at-least-7b.

The media companies that control the broadcasts of college football games know that the money paid to each of the conferences is a source of power and can lead to the exploitation of college football. We will see the impact of that money and its manipulative effect throughout this book.

CHAPTER 8

"Without a doubt, July 2021 was when the first domino fell," a Pac-12 insider told us. "Some of us believed it at that, that this thing was going to spiral out of control. Some of us took it as minor news in comparison to the NIL law that had passed a few weeks earlier. It's pretty clear a few years later who took which stance when that news dropped."

On July 22, 2021, an ESPN broadcast went live, and the news ran rampant across all media platforms.

Stephen A. Smith reported:

> *According to a report yesterday in the Houston Chronicle, Texas and Oklahoma have reached out to the SEC about joining the conference with an announcement in the coming weeks.*

Let me be clear: this is a very good day if you're a fan of Oklahoma and Texas.

That means the SEC, the best conference, the most passionate fan bases. Of course Oklahoma and Texas want a piece of that! Of course they want to position themselves as one of the programs competing for spots in the future 12-team playoff.

But man... It's a horrible day for the rest of the Big 12. For the rest of college sports. Because it's about to be the SEC vs. everybody else.

There were 129 FBS programs (now 134), and the SEC isn't going to take all of them. Oklahoma and Texas are just getting in while they still can.

The rest of college football outside the SEC will have to figure things out for themselves.
Good luck with that.

Several factors led to this move, with financial incentives and competitive advantages at the forefront. The SEC's commitment to excellence was further magnified when it overcame the COVID hurdle and cemented itself as the power conference in college football. Under Commissioner Sankey, the conference only furthered the growth of a brand that had become synonymous with football excellence.

After the COVID debacle and NIL legislation, the sport seemed in flux. On the horizon, the next wave of seismic shifts loomed, predicated on the ability to remember two things about college football teams:

1. Football teams are comprised of players. The best teams land the best players. Stick with me here.

2. Teams belong to conferences. If teams can buy the best players, what happens when a conference is "bought?" Thanks to the 1984 lawsuit initiated by... none other than... Oklahoma, conferences were controlled by the few large media entities that negotiated media rights for the majority of the power conferences.

When media rights don't tie a team down, there's some fluidity to what they can do. Before 2021, when a conference's media rights were expiring, teams were the equivalent of "restricted free agents." If a team wanted to leave their conference, there needed to be a desire on the team's part to leave, a desire on at least one conference's part to fight for their membership, and most importantly, a financial incentive. Since the dawn of long-term media rights deals, teams have viewed the window before the end of a term as the time to test the waters, take or make calls, and see what options are out there.

In May 1990, the SEC presidents voted to authorize expansion with ACC (Atlantic Coast Conference) powerhouse South Carolina and Arkansas of the Southwestern Conference (the SWC eventually merged with the Big Eight Conference to form the Big 12 in 1996). This marked the birth of two divisions within the SEC and the introduction of a "conference championship" game, which proved to be incredibly advantageous in the '90s toward crowning the best team in college football.

Through the years, media companies saw just how profitable college football was. To use a business term, they began "rolling up" independents like Penn State, which was added to the Big Ten in 1990. The ACC joined in on the fun and landed Florida State as an anchor tenant to their conference in 1990 as well. In 2003, the ACC picked off Miami from the Big East, as well as Virginia Tech. Boston College would join the ACC a year later.

Now that these "realignment" phases were starting to become more predictable, conference and media figureheads began anxiously anticipating these windows. The window in the early 2010s showed what intense reshuffling could be done.

The Big Ten Council of Presidents determined in December 2009 that they were ready to be the big winner in the next era, so much so that they published an unprompted announcement to their commissioner requesting "recommendations for consideration over the next 12 to 18 months." They ended up bringing in Nebraska in June 2010 to sit at 12 teams.

Meanwhile, on the West Coast, something was brewing...

New Commissioner Larry Scott (sound familiar?) had been appointed to lead the now-Pac-10 (Arizona and Arizona State were added to the Pac-8 in 1978) in the early 2010s. Early on, he tried to do something similar to what the Big 12 had done: bite off a chunk of another conference and combine it with his own. The glorious Pac-16 conference concept was set to unite the Southwest with the West Coast and dominate college football.

Commissioner Scott was prepared to take on Texas, Texas A&M, Oklahoma, Oklahoma State, Texas Tech, and Colorado. Although Colorado accepted, Scott had a wild turn of events where the deal was on, then it was off, and then it was back on, but eventually, this proposal fell through. Scott was able to bring on Utah as the travel partner to Colorado and formed the Pac-12. That was a success at the time, and life went on.

Little did the Pac-12 know what was on the horizon...

Beyond the Pac-10 becoming the Pac-12, the SEC hit Texas A&M and Missouri with a promotion from the Big 12 and expanded to 14 teams in the summer of 2011. TCU and West Virginia were brought up from the Mountain West and Big East, respectively, to compete in the Big 12 conference. By the fall of 2011, Pittsburgh, Louisville, and Syracuse came into the ACC from the Big East, while Notre Dame came in and agreed to compete in a partial football scheduling agreement with the ACC. The Big Ten scooped up who they wanted early on, but some would argue they were getting outperformed in the "conference arms race." The Big Ten acted quickly and secured the media markets of New York and Washington, DC, adding Maryland and Rutgers.

In these waves of realignment, it's essential to act swiftly and decisively, whether it's the right move or not (the Big Ten gets crushed for having Maryland and Rutgers, as they drastically underperform year after year). As Commissioner Delaney of the Big Ten put it, "We came to the conclusion there was more risk sitting still than there was exploring other opportunities."[1] That philosophy proved to be the guiding light to the promised land, which included consistent playoff berths and several championships. For those who opted in favor of inaction, the strategy spelled their downfall.

Whether it was the right move for the sake of competitive matchups or better viewership, Commissioner Delaney knew one thing: bad news doesn't get better over time. It's too bad a commissioner of a different conference—and his successor, both of whom had zero experience in college athletics—didn't study the success of college football conference leaders like Delaney. In the modern age of television, media, and rapid information distribution, it's baffling that this message didn't travel from the East Coast to the West Coast. For Pac-12 fans who cherish history, rivalry, and traditions forged over the last century, this ignorance of consecutive commissioners would prove to be costly.

Take note of the pattern here, though: slowly but surely, consolidation persists throughout the CFB landscape. The tectonic plates slowly shift... awaiting the next eruption.

This pattern reached a new crescendo with the announcement of the SEC's groundbreaking media rights deal in December 2020. As conference politics intensified during the COVID period, ESPN saw that the SEC was bulletproof. Not even a global shutdown could hurt the conference. The hierarchy of power among the Power Five conferences became even more pronounced post-COVID. The incompe-

---

1. Jim Delany, quoted in *Yahoo Sports*, "College Football Conference Realignment History," November 2012, https://sports.yahoo.com/college-football-conference-realignment-history-100132966.html.

of Kevin Warren and the fearful approach of Larry Scott sent the signal to ESPN to push all their chips in on the SEC.

Not only did ESPN lock down the best football conference, but they *knew* they had the most powerful brand in college football. With that comes tremendous leverage, so why not shake things up? This was the best time to do it, and teams were shell-shocked coming out of COVID-19, trying to understand how they were supposed to get back to normal.

In college football, as we've seen, when there is a major global event, the sport is affected. Now we had the culmination of COVID-19, coupled with the first approvals to legalize paying players.

Just as the sport had found some stability in conference alignment, feathers were ruffled in a way that rivaled the eras when there was legislation to ban football and World War II taking place.

This time, however, it came right before... the next media rights negotiating window.

CHAPTER 9

"When able to attack, we must seem unable; when using our forces, we must seem inactive; when we are near, we must make the enemy believe we are far away; when far away, we must make him believe we are near."

This is the essence of Sun Tzu's *The Art of War*, the manual on the intricate dance of strategy. Sun Tzu lived from 544 BC to 496 BC, and his focus was on the power of preparation, the importance of adaptability, and the need for mastery of deception. He taught that the greatest victories are achieved without fighting. Instead, they are gained through the manipulation of the enemy's perception and a careful analysis of circumstances.

Sun Tzu emphasized the fluidity of war, stressing that rigidity leads to defeat, while those who master the art of flexibility will dominate the battlefield. His doctrine was less about brute force and more about the intelligent application of strategy, turning the tides of conflict through insight and foresight. The core tenets of surprise, misdirection, and psychological warfare are what make Sun Tzu's teachings timeless, applicable not just to war but to any competitive arena where the stakes are high and the margin for error is thin.

As we've seen throughout history, anticipation is great when a competitive landscape grows and gets more complex. For instance, there's a different buzz around college football when the media rights negotiation period approaches. Whether it's due to COVID-19 kick-starting division in the United States or an event like Texas and Oklahoma abandoning their conference and joining forces with the SEC, tension always seems to rise as significant events are on the horizon.

The buzz was alive and well more than thirty months before rights grants were extended to conference members. With Texas and Oklahoma headed for a new home, the SEC and ESPN were more stable than ever, having already secured their teams, media agreements, and, of course, financial stability.

So, what did the Big 12 have to say about all this? This is a conference we haven't talked about much up to this point. Their approach is worth a look, as it was very different from the aforementioned conferences. The Big 12 had been awfully quiet up to this point, but losing its anchor tenants to a league that had been running laps around it in most major statistics called for a "code red". As ESPN declined their request for a TV deal years in advance, Big 12 Commissioner Bob Bowlsby asked repeatedly for an explanation of why the teams needed to leave. "To this day, [Texas and Oklahoma have] given us no answers to that question. I've asked repeatedly, and they never made us aware of any concerns in advance. When we've asked the question since then, we've gotten no response."[1]

Commissioner Bowlsby needed to take action. And he knew that.

"We [the Big 12] expect to lead on the playing surfaces, in the classroom, and in steering and strengthening intercollegiate athletics in '21 and '22 and beyond."[2]

To his credit, it took just one week for the "loss" to be turned into a note addressed to ESPN's president of programming and original content, Burke Magnus.

Here's what came across Magnus's desk:

July 28, 2021
Burke Magnus
ESPN, Inc.
President, Programming and Original Content

Dear Burke:

It has come to my direct attention that ESPN, the current business partner of the Big 12 Conference, has taken certain actions that are intended to not only harm the Big 12 Conference but to result in financial benefits for ESPN. It has come to my direct

---

1. Bob Bowlsby, quoted in *Heartland College Sports*, "Bob Bowlsby Says Texas, Oklahoma Departure 'Personal Betrayal,'" October 20, 2021
   https://www.heartlandcollegesports.com/2021/10/20/bob-bowlsby-says-texas-oklahoma-departure-personal-betrayal-report/.
2. Bowlsby, "Texas, Oklahoma Departure 'Personal Betrayal.'"

attention that ESPN, the current business partner of the Big 12 Conference, has taken certain actions that are intended to not only harm the Big 12 Conference but also result in financial benefits for ESPN. Setting aside ESPN's potential involvement in the recent announcement by the University of Texas and the University of Oklahoma that they intend to leave the Big 12 Conference in 2025 (as to which we reserve all legal rights), I am aware that ESPN has also been actively engaged in discussions with at least one other conference regarding that conference inducing additional Members of the Big 12 Conference to leave the Big 12 Conference.

As you know, our Members have entered into contractual obligations to the Big 12 Conference under the Amended and Restated Agreement related to the grant to the Conference of the rights to televise their athletic events (the "Grant of Rights Agreement").

The actions noted above are an apparent attempt to interfere with and to induce our Members to breach these contractual obligations to the Conference and to encourage further conference realignment for the financial benefit of ESPN.

Further, as you also know, Section 20.2 (c) of the Amended the Restated Agreement between the Big 12 Conference and ESPN (the *Telecast Agreement) states that ESPN will not "take any actions likely to impair, or [that are] inconsistent with, the rights Conference has acquired under this Agreement. ESPN acknowledges that the Conference's rights herein are valuable, *specific, and unique." ESPN's recent actions also violate, at a minimum, Section 20.2(c) of the Telecast Agreement.*

The Big 12 Conference demands that ESPN immediately cease and desist all actions that may harm the Conference and its members and that it not communicate with the Big 12 Conference's existing Members or any other NCAA Conference regarding the Big 12 Conference's Members, possible conference realignment, or potential financial incentives or outcomes related to possible conference realignment.
The Big 12 Conference reserves and will enforce all of its rights under the Grant of Rights Agreement and the Telecast Agreement to the full extent of the law and will not allow its business to be interfered with by its business partners or others. Please provide the Big 12 Conference with your written assurances that all such actions will immediately cease and desist by noon Central Time on July 29, 2021.

Sincerely,
Robert A. Bowlsby, II
Commissioner

As the Big 12 sat on life support, the other three major conferences were forming a plan of their own for survival. After rumblings of potential realignment, all of it was put to rest (or so we thought...) on August 24, 2021, when the news broke:

Forty-one world-class institutions across three of the Power Five conferences agreed to collaborate on the future evolution of college athletics and the Inter-Conference Scheduling Alliance.

That's right. As the SEC remained stable and the Big 12 seemed headed for oblivion, the other three Power Five conferences decided they would band together. Aligning themselves with each other was their response to the SEC's consolidation of the most prominent programs in college sports.

"The ACC, Big Ten, and Pac-12 recognize the unique environment and challenges currently facing intercollegiate athletics, and we are proud and confident in this timely and necessary alliance that brings together like-minded institutions and conferences focused on the overall educational missions of our preeminent institutions," said ACC Commissioner Jim Phillips. "The alliance will ensure that the educational outcomes and experiences for student-athletes participating at the highest level of collegiate athletics will remain the driving factor in all decisions moving forward."

Big Ten Commissioner Kevin Warren appeared ecstatic when announcing the alliance (almost as ecstatic as his announcement canceling the season due to COVID a year earlier): "Today, through this alliance, we furthered our commitment to our student-athletes by prioritizing our academics and athletics value systems. We are creating opportunities for student-athletes to have elite competition and are taking the necessary steps to shape and stabilize the future of college athletics."

Newly hired Pac-12 Commissioner George Kliavkoff had spent less than two months on the job when the alliance was announced. "The historic alliance announced today between the Pac-12, ACC, and Big Ten is grounded in a commitment to our student-athletes. We believe that by collaborating together, we are stronger in our commitment to addressing the broad issues and opportunities facing college athletics."[3]

Post-game press conferences are notorious for being riddled with mundane and predictable talk. If you win big, it goes something like, "We played great. Really proud of our guys for executing all week and seeing it work out on game day." After a loss, it typically goes something like, "Frustrating loss. Credit to them, they were the better team. We've got to get better."

It's rare for a coach or player to stray from this common verbiage. In fact, when a high-ranking professional in sports does, the clip has the potential to go viral on major news shows and generate buzz on social media. The increased publicity and media expansion around sports have made these press relations events more predictable and boring.

When I first saw this news about an alliance of three major conferences, I was very intrigued. Were the conferences going to merge under one branding and name? Was this a scheduling agreement to eliminate meaningless non-conference and FCS games that bore most fans to death as their team triumphs to a 58–0 victory in front of a sparse home crowd in the late summer weeks? Or was this just some meaningless virtue signal that tries to say, "Hey, fans? Just wanted to

---

3. George Kliavkoff, quoted in "ACC, Big Ten, and Pac-12 Announce Historic Alliance," *TheACC.com*, August 24, 2021,
  https://theacc.com/news/2021/8/24/general-acc-big-ten-and-pac-12-announce-historic-alliance.aspx.

let you know we care." I saw the term "strategic alliance," which seemed promising, but I had to wonder *What exactly are they going to do?"* As I watched these press conferences and read comments, I heard what sounded like "coach speak" at a post-game press conference.

Go back and read those quotes from the conference commissioners.

They're talking in platitudes.

The hope was that the alliance would include more competitive matchups across the leagues, but Ohio State AD Gene Smith stated clearly to ESPN, "We have a plan when it comes to football scheduling... and we won't change that plan. We won't put a burden on our [Big Ten] teams to have to play an ACC or a Pac-12 opponent on an annual basis."[4]

Hmmm. A conflict of interest? Involuntary obligations?

These ADs, chancellors, commissioners, and coaches have all come together with great intentions but without a true...plan to do anything in the near term. Perhaps they wouldn't do anything because it would make too much sense? ACC commissioner Jim Phillips also made it clear, after some time in the alliance, that "we [as an alliance] have had some success—maybe not to the level that the general public wants, but if you look at just the complexities of overall scheduling, we have had some pretty good progress."[5]

---

4. Gene Smith, quoted in "The Alliance Explained: ACC, Big Ten and Pac-12 on CFP Vote, Scheduling and What Comes Next," *ESPN*, February 2022, https://www.espn.com/college-football/story/_/id/33413775/the-alliance-explained-acc-big-ten-pac-12-cfp-vote-scheduling-comes-next.
5. Phillips, "The Alliance Explained."

Translation: What we are doing is working. You won't see any indicators, but rest assured, our alliance is being enforced and working perfectly.

Florida AD Scott Stricklin confirmed that he saw this agreement the same way. "It appeared to be a response to OU and Texas," Stricklin said. "I'm not sure if it was an effort to stabilize or if it was a defensive gesture." Stricklin wasn't alone, as those on the outside remained skeptical about Alliance matchups.

"You don't need an alliance for that," another Power Five athletic director said. "I promise you some of them aren't interested in scheduling each other like that; otherwise, they could have been doing it all along." I revisited the press conference a few weeks after I began my dig into understanding this... "alliance" of sorts.

That's when I saw it.

The master of military science in ancient China and the creator of the military doctrine regarding asymmetrical warfare spoke almost specifically about this 2,500 years ago. I was shocked when I read the passage. It all finally made sense.

> *"When the general is weak and without authority;*
> *when his orders are not clear and distinct;*
> *when there are no fixed duties assigned to officers and men,*
> *and the ranks are formed in a slovenly, haphazard manner,*
> *the result is utter disorganization."*

2,500 years later...

Kliavkoff: "I'm okay with there not being a signed contract... We didn't focus on that. We didn't even talk about that."

Warren: "We have a responsibility to our future generations to do what's right."

(As if canceling the 2020 season was "right." Nice one, KW.)

Jim Phillips, regarding the lack of a signed document: "It's about trust. We've looked each other in the eye and made an agreement."

Kliavkoff: "There's no signed document, and there doesn't need to be."[6]

So, how did this fare?

---

6. Kevin Warren, Jim Phillips, and George Kliavkoff, quoted in "Big Ten, ACC, Pac-12 Commissioners Weigh In on the Alliance, SEC and CFP Expansion and Where the Big 12 Stands," *Eleven Warriors*, August 24, 2021, https://www.elevenwarriors.com/college-football/2021/08/124296/big-ten-acc-pac-12-commissioners-weigh-in-on-the-alliance-sec-and-cfp-expansion-and-where-the-big-12-stands.

CHAPTER 10

The Texas and Oklahoma departures from the Big 12 set off a chain reaction that drastically restructured college football in ways no one could have predicted. This one move sent shockwaves through the college athletics landscape, leaving the conference at eight teams and scrambling to regain its footing after losing two of its revenue-generating powerhouses.

The remaining eight teams were:

Texas Christian University (TCU Horned Frogs)

- **Media Market:** Dallas-Fort Worth, TX
- **Market Rank:** 5th

West Virginia University (West Virginia Mountaineers)

- **Media Market:** Pittsburgh, PA (also serves Morgantown, WV, area)
- **Market Rank:** 26th

University of Kansas (Kansas Jayhawks)

- **Media Market:** Kansas City, KS/MO
- **Market Rank:** 32nd

Kansas State University (Kansas State Wildcats)

- **Media Market:** Manhattan, KS (also serves Kansas City, KS/MO area)
- **Market Rank:** 32nd (Kansas City, KS/MO)

Oklahoma State University (Oklahoma State Cowboys)

- **Media Market:** Tulsa, OK (serves Stillwater, OK)
- **Market Rank:** 63rd

Iowa State University (Iowa State Cyclones)

- **Media Market:** Des Moines, IA
- **Market Rank:** 68th

Baylor University (Baylor Bears)

- **Media Market:** Waco, TX
- **Market Rank:** 87th

Texas Tech University (Texas Tech Red Raiders)

- **Media Market:** Lubbock, TX
- **Market Rank:** 145th

We confirmed that in the summer of 2021, Kliavkoff began receiving calls from Big 12 schools looking for a new home. In fact, he and Commissioner Bowlsby went through a series of discussions and even met in person to discuss a unified league that would include most of the twenty best programs west of the Mississippi River (along with West Virginia, which, though east of the Mississippi, competed in the Big Twelve). Presumably, the Pac-12 would welcome an alliance of sorts with the Big 12, as they would have a team in every time zone and unite major programs across the country against the SEC.

But remember, the alliance between the Big Ten, Pac-12, and ACC didn't have any clauses defining how expansion would affect specific teams.

Could the Big 12 be welcomed into the fold, turning college football on its head with two superleagues?

Would the other three conferences in the alliance have to approve this?

What about expansion clauses?

Was expanding the alliance seen as betrayal or as contributing to the greater good?

Did the alliance even want to expand?

Did the alliance even...exist functionally?

Well, when you have an agreement with nothing in writing, you leave plenty of room for interpretation.

None of the alliance members agreed to clauses and parameters about any of this. In fact, the alliance didn't have any clauses on... anything. Remember, "there's no signed document, and there doesn't need to be."

With or without a formal agreement from the alliance, Kliavkoff saw the opportunity to join forces with the Big 12. He promptly formed an expansion committee consisting of members from his conference to discuss how this would work. When Kliavkoff was hired, the intent was that he would unite all parties and lead the conference back to prominence by showing schools genuine concern and unwavering loyalty from the league office.

So, how did he handle this situation? There's a lot on the table.

"I want to go on record and say that the Pac-12 is in favor of both the expansion of the College Football Playoff's four teams and the implementation of consistent guidelines for name, image, and likeness," Kliavkoff said during his introductory news conference. "We think that both CFB expansion and NIL legislation are good for college sports fans, good for our student-athletes, and can be a significant competitive advantage for the Pac-12."[1]

He's right. But there was one glaring issue.

Kliavkoff graduated from the University of Virginia School of Law and held prominent positions with Major League Baseball, NBCUniversal, and MGM Resorts International. Before joining the Pac-12, Kliavkoff was the president of entertainment and sports at MGM Resorts International in Las Vegas. During his tenure, he served on several boards, including those of the T-Mobile Arena and Cirque du Soleil. He also represented the Las Vegas Aces on the WNBA's Board of Governors, overseeing the sale of the Aces to Las Vegas Raiders owner Mark Davis in 2021. His extensive experience in media included a key role in launching Hulu during his time at NBCUniversal.

Kliavkoff had a diverse background, but he had never handled media rights negotiations for institutional athletics. He also had no experience with conference politics, west coast universities, or anything in the college athletics space.

Hiring an outsider can work out tremendously, but it's a high-risk, high-reward situation. In this case, the risk was gargantuan.

Things had already been going downhill throughout Larry Scott's tenure. Let's look at 2018, year nine of Scott's tenure. This was a

---

1. George Kliavkoff, quoted in Chris Karpman, "Five Takeaways: Introduction of New Pac-12 Commissioner George Kliavkoff," *247Sports*, May 13, 2021,
   https://247sports.com/college/arizona-state/Article/George-Kliavkoff-Pac-12-Networks-commissioner-Arizona-State-football-NIL-legislation-NCAA-CFP-expansion-165366721/.

disastrous year for the Pac-12. The conference started the year fresh off a 1–8 record in football bowl games, then proceeded to go winless in March Madness. There was also an instant replay scandal, which never helps the sport or its credibility. The Pac-12 Network, launched by Scott, filled less than 20 million homes in the U.S. It got so bad that the conference was caught in an attempt to pay the *LA Times* for positive news coverage. Meanwhile, the Midwest and Southeastern Conferences thrived, sending forward champion after champion across all sports.

Even USC, the Pac-12's largest brand historically, scurried to a 4–5 finish. Oregon, with all its glitz and glam, barely finished with a winning season. UCLA brought in Chip Kelly in an attempt to return his magic to the Pac-12, only to field an abysmal 3–9 squad in front of sparsely attended home games at the Rose Bowl. The Pac-12 called itself the "Conference of Champions" since its teams and athletes had won the most championships across all sports. However, an important asterisk should go next to this moniker. The Pac-12 had run up its numbers in several Olympic sports. These are crucial to having a well-rounded athletic department, sure, but financially, only two sports matter: football and basketball. In Scott's seven years in the CFP era, the Pac-12 fielded just two semifinal teams, Oregon in 2014 and Washington in 2016, neither of which emerged as champions. In contrast, the Big Ten was represented four times with one national champion, and the SEC put forth seven teams in that period, four of which emerged as champions.

In 2020, Scott announced that he would be taking a pay reduction. Rightfully so, due to his conference's abysmal performance. What he failed to mention? He happily accepted a $2.2 million bonus while about half his staff were laid off or furloughed in 2020 due to the COVID pandemic. That year, after half of his workforce was sent home, Scott brought in a walloping $5.3 million. On salary. As conference commissioner. This is more than what his SEC and Big Ten counterparts made *combined*.

Finally, the Pac-12 presidents and chancellors gave in to what the fans had been begging for and brought in a gentleman with a clean slate. Gambling on an outsider to save a conference that is actively in freefall is not the best move, but Kliavkoff is who they wanted.

So, re-enter Kliavkoff, who remained open to the idea of taking all eight of the remaining Big 12 schools to survive the hectic summer of 2021. However, he expressed more interest in poaching the top schools of the Big 12 and sending the rest to find a home elsewhere. His expansion committee of six officials, each representing two schools (their travel pairings).

When the committee met in 2021, USC President Carol Folt represented USC and UCLA. One woman was representing two of the largest brands in the conference, *and* the second-largest media market in the country. After a significant announcement took place the next year in June 2022, Folt went silent. She refused to speak about what the committee had discussed.

That will all be very important to this story. But we aren't there yet.

So let's return to the Pac-12 expansion committee meeting in the summer of 2021.

When it came to the possibility of a Big 12/Pac-12 merger, Folt was the first to speak up. Again, though she refused to comment publicly, we have internally confirmed the following details:

1. The officials at the Pac-12 conference prepared a presentation that broke down expansion and what that would entail.
2. No more than 15 minutes in, Folt pushed back on the whole proposal, questioning why the conference was even considering expansion.

When the representative of the two most powerful brands in your conference—the ones controlling the largest media market by a mile—speaks up in a room like this, you pause, listen, and then survey the landscape. The strategy is clear in theory: gather your intel, survey the battlefield, and then lay out your plan. Whether it's Sun Tzu, linebacker Lawrence Taylor, or Navy SEAL Jocko Willink, the wisdom is the same: understand the terrain before making your move.

George Kliavkoff was supposed to be the conference's savior. He *had* to be the conference's savior as the one brought in to clean up the mess left behind by Larry Scott.

This was *his* moment, the first real chance for the Pac-12 to show that it belonged and forge a partnership with the desperate Big 12. He was hired to pull together a group of schools with wildly different agendas. Now was his time to shine: to bolster his conference, dominate the next decade, and go out on his own terms.

For someone tasked with "uniting all parties", Kliavkoff's first move should've been to listen to all parties—or, given that he held all the cards, to explain his plans and intentions and then listen to everyone else's opinion.

But then came the silence.

"A lot of times, the way these president rooms work," a source confided to the *LA Times*, "the person who speaks loudest and first sets the dynamic."

"And if there's no one with a strong enough knowledge base or the guts to challenge it, well, they just go along. They assume that person knows what they're doing."[2]

GROUPTHINK.

Kliavkoff needed to rise to the occasion.

Instead, he chose not to push back against USC's Carol Folt, seeing the leverage USC held over the league. The meeting ended soon after, with Kliavkoff signaling to the Big 12 that the Pac-12 wasn't interested in expanding at all.

A decision that mimicked a fatal mistake from 2011 when the Pac-12 passed on expanding to 16 teams. Less than a year later, in June 2022, the conference would be blindsided by a move that made Folt's resistance to expansion all too clear.

Kliavkoff, like Folt, declined to comment.

---

2. J. Brady McCollough, "Inside the Pac-12's Decision to Postpone the 2020 Football Season," *Los Angeles Times*, August 11, 2020, https://www.latimes.com/sports/story/2020-08-11/pac-12-decision-postpone-2020-football-season.

Remember the cease-and-desist that the Big 12 sent ESPN about manipulating college football and threatening the conference's existence? Well, the Big 12 was right about this ESPN collusion. There's a common theme throughout this debacle: the Big 12 was right about a lot.

Had ESPN's master plan worked and had Kliavkoff listened to the rest of his room, the Big 12 would have likely merged with the Pac-12. This made tremendous sense for most parties. Yes, the Big 12 would get screwed, but that was what the networks wanted. Barring over-the-top savvy and finesse, the networks always get what they want. A Pac-12 insider told us, "Credit to the Big 12; they saw through everything that ESPN tried to do and fought resiliently."

"But everything stopped when the Pac-12 shut down the merger, though. Those (TV) guys thought, 'Hmmm... maybe the Pac-12 is the one that could fall?'"

Savvy and finesse kept the Big 12 conference going.

But what happens to a conference with horrendous management?

Kliavkoff stood to benefit from having this explained to him.

Let's take a look at the conferences' media alignments. These were the Power Five conferences at the time:

- Big Ten
- SEC
- ACC
- Big 12
- Pac-12

WHERE DID OUR GAME GO?

Here were their media allegiances moving forward:

- Big Ten: Primarily Fox, with CBS and NBC secondarily through 2030
- SEC: Exclusively ESPN through 2033
- ACC: Exclusively ESPN through 2036*

*Unilateral clause from the network's side.

The Big 12 and Pac-12 did not receive deals in advance, while the SEC and Big Ten did.

Let me know if you see a pattern in these deals as of 2021.

- Big 12: ESPN/Fox (slight advantage to ESPN, as they receive 12/20 as well as football and basketball championship games).
- Pac-12: Fox and ESPN split marquee matchups, with the 100% conference-owned Pac-12 Network getting the marquee matchup a few times per year.

Did it click for you? As the networks took control of the game, it *made sense* for the Big 12 and the Pac-12 to merge. Merging makes for newer and better conference matchups, translating to higher viewership and, most importantly, more profit for Fox and ESPN.

Fox, through the Big Ten, had been fighting for Texas for years, but the SEC (ESPN) gave the Longhorns a better deal and ensured that their rivalry with Oklahoma remained intact.

Once these terms were outlined, Texas and Oklahoma left.

Now, if you look at those allegiances, you could say that ESPN has two whole leagues: the ACC and the SEC. And if the ACC's contract is longer, then why wouldn't those two conferences just merge to guarantee their stability for longer?

Well, there's an asterisk by the ACC.

Just because they're secured through 2036 doesn't mean they're safe.

There is an option listed in the 2016 ACC Tier I Agreement that grants ESPN the unilateral right to leave the ACC altogether in 2027, leaving the conference with zero media backing.

Remember, the best players go to the best teams. The best teams go to the best conferences, which exist because media networks give them the most money.

But, no media backing = no big payout = opportunity for big programs to leave the conference.

So, by 2027, ESPN will decide whether to carry the ACC on the network. If ESPN opts not to extend the agreement, the major programs could push to leave the conference. We have already seen this play out in the 2023–2024 offseason with a disgruntled Florida State, which missed the playoffs in favor of one-loss teams from other conferences. The CFP committee cited the strength of schedule and deemed other conferences more competitive.

Want to know what Kliavkoff thought of all this?

When pressed about the "kill or be killed" nature of college conferences, he said at his own media day on July 21, 2023, "Our schools are committed to each other and the Pac-12. We'll get our media rights deal done. We'll announce the deal. I think the realignment going on in college athletics will come to an end."

Want to know what the networks had in mind?

- Big 12 (Fox/ESPN) received four schools from the Pac-12 (Fox/ESPN)
- ACC (ESPN) received two schools from the Pac-12 (Fox/ESPN)
- Big Ten (FOX) received four schools from Pac-12 (Fox/ESPN)
- SEC (ESPN) received two schools from the Big 12 (Fox/ESPN)

The schools that the Big Ten received are much more storied in terms of success and prestige. The University of Washington, Oregon, USC, and UCLA all joined the Big Ten, while Arizona, Arizona State, Utah, and Colorado joined the Big 12. After consulting with experts in the field, both ESPN and FOX were not only satisfied with what they received but were estimated to have received equal gain.

Taking the approach that no one will poach your schools in the midst of media rights instability showcases a great degree of delusion and hubris.

Where were his advisors? Where were his ADs and chancellors?

One of Sun Tzu's most famous quotes: "If the enemy leaves a door open, you must rush in."

The Big 12, seeing this unfold, perked up and opted to take a drastically different approach than the Pac-12, perhaps drawing upon this bit of Sun Tzu's wisdom.

CHAPTER 11

Commissioner Bowlsby of the Big 12 conference had been tasked with the impossible. After fighting day in and day out, it looked like he and his conference could make it out alive... and maybe even ahead.

What was the silver lining to Texas and Oklahoma's departure?

"They lobbied against Big 12 expansion heavily," Bowlsby said. "The more our group became committed to one another and moving forward with the group of eight, the more we began to believe adding additional members made good sense."

Bowlsby had been part of the earlier vetting process when the Big 12 considered expanding then pulled back. This time, though, he knew these schools were ready, as was he.

This was a move that needed to be done for the sake of survival. Sharks were swarming.

Could the Big 12, the underdog in this story, defy the odds and walk away stronger? While the Pac-12 caught a case of analysis paralysis, the Big 12 set its sights on several top media markets, starting just south of Salt Lake City.

For BYU, getting into the Big 12 was the end of a long road they'd been traveling for years. Cougars AD Tom Holmoe said, "Six years ago, some saw it as a failure when we didn't get into the Big 12."

"But at that point, our coaches, student-athletes, and administration made a commitment that this wasn't going to be a failure—it would be a launching point." Holmoe continued, "The last six years haven't been about a full-court press, but rather a constant, collective effort to make this happen."[1]

The addition of BYU brought the Big 12 up to nine teams.

UCF, as we discussed earlier, was coming off the wildest two-year turnaround in college football history. Remember, 0–12 in 2015. The only undefeated FBS team in 2017,[2] They were eyeing a move to a Power Five conference as well. Athletic Director Terry Mohajir, who took the reins in February 2021, made this his top priority. "Putting

---

1. Tom Holmoe, quoted in Jay Drew, "When the Time Came, We Were Ready: Tom Holmoe Deserves Props for Keeping BYU's Power Five Hopes Alive," *Deseret News*, September 10, 2021, https://www.deseret.com/2021/9/10/22667330/byu-big-12-invite-admitted-tom-holmoe-bob-bowlsby-joining-in-2023-houston-ucf-cincinnati/.
2. The NCAA officially recognizes UCF as the 2017 national champion alongside the CFP champion Alabama. The Colley Matrix ranked the Knights #1 in the country, which was claimed by the university following this announcement and now appears in the official NCAA records.

our athletics program in a position to move to a power conference was so important that I began making calls on my second day on the job."[3]

A couple of months before the news broke about Texas and Oklahoma's move to the SEC, Mohajir laid out a long-term strategy for UCF's athletics to President Alexander Cartwright, who was remarkably supportive.

"Sometimes you get lucky," Cartwright said, "but you have to be prepared to get lucky, and we were prepared."[4]

"It just so happened that the gates opened up, and we were there," Mohajir added.

Now they sat at ten teams in the conference.

Two days after University of Cincinnati officials confirmed that the school had submitted its application to join the Big 12, the conference's board of directors voted to extend a membership invitation to them. The Bearcats own a special spot in history as the only non-power five team to EVER earn a spot in the College Football Playoff under the four-team model. (Power 5 includes ACC, Big 10, Big 12, Pac 12, and SEC)

---

3. Terry Mohajir, "Terry Mohajir on UCF's Journey to the Big 12," *University of Central Florida News*, July 13, 2023,, https://www.ucf.edu/news/terry-mohajir-on-ucfs-journey-to-the-big-12/.
4. Alexander Cartwright, quoted in "Big 12 Votes to Accept Adding BYU, Cincinnati, Houston, UCF to Conference," *ESPN*, September 10, 2021, https://www.espn.com/college-football/story/_/id/32182361/big-12-votes-accept-adding-byu-cincinnati-houston-ucf-conference.

"The Big 12 invitation only confirms our core belief: UC has earned its seat at the Power Five table," Cincinnati President Neville Pinto said.

Boom. That's number eleven for the Big 12.

Securing the markets of Orlando (16th), Salt Lake City (27th), and Cincinnati (37th) bolstered the strength of this new-age Big 12.

The cherry on top, however, was the basketball powerhouse that sat in the sixth-ranked media market.

"The trajectory and growth of the University of Houston in recent years are undeniable. We are prepared for this moment, ready to compete, and excited about what the Cougars will bring to the Big 12 Conference," said Tilman Fertitta, Chairman of the UH Board of Regents. "This is a proud moment in UH history. We are humbled, honored, excited, and ready to get to work. Together, what we can accomplish is limitless."

And just like that, the new and improved Big 12 had been rebuilt with new teams and much stronger media markets. They were now *Big*. And for a moment... they were finally back to 12.[5]

Remember the strategic alliance that was intended to change college athletics in ways we couldn't have imagined? Bowlsby, who had defied the odds and kept his conference alive, was asked about this in an interview with ESPN.

---

5. For one season, they were up to 14 teams until Texas and Oklahoma left.

"I think the reason that we weren't included was probably twofold," he said.

"One was that they didn't want to be accused of collusion by having all four conferences seeming to gang up on the SEC. And the other was [the Big 12] was in a state of somewhat disarray."[6]

Commissioner Bowlsby spoke with honesty after gearing up for another successful era in Big 12 athletics. He paused before adding what we all now see clearly:

"I don't really look at ourselves as being on the outside looking in simply because we don't know what [the alliance] is going to be."[7]

And that was it. They didn't know. Hindsight is 20/20, and it's hard to predict when something is false. Now we know that the alliance wasn't anything real. It was a smokescreen, a diversion, an empty vessel designed to look like power. Behind the carefully crafted statements and mutual assurances was a void—no vision, no plan, just desperation.

Jump over to the Big Ten. They were cooking something serious. Kevin Warren needed to redeem himself after his COVID clusterfunk. Warren created a group that one person described as "an expansion subcommittee" consisting of conference administrators to explore adding teams. As one Big Ten source told us, "Something has to

---

6. Bob Bowlsby, quoted in Heather Dinich, "Big 12's Bob Bowlsby Says Conference's Exclusion from Alliance Was 'Probably Two-Fold'," *ESPN*, August 25, 2021, https://www.espn.com/college-football/story/_/id/32081292/big-12-bob-bowlsby-says-conference-exclusion-alliance-was-probably-two-fold.
7. Bowlsby, "Big 12's Bob Bowlsby Says Conference's Exclusion."

happen to combat the Texas and Oklahoma move. Otherwise, the SEC would eventually eat up the Big Ten."

Warren's job? To ensure it was **two** conferences at the top. His alongside the SEC.

Remember USC President Carol Folt lobbying against Pac-12 expansion and then not saying a word? Well, June 30, 2022, would explain everything.

That's when the bombshell hit.

USC and UCLA—two of the bedrocks of college football on the West Coast—were abandoning the Pac-12 for the Big Ten. Suddenly, the alliance that supposedly "united" these institutions was exposed. It was all a façade.

The other universities in the Pac-12 were stunned. How long had USC and UCLA been scheming behind closed doors? How long had the Pac-12 been a house of cards, waiting for a stiff wind to blow it down? The LA schools didn't even have the decency to go quietly. No, they went to the **Big Ten**, stretching their footprint from Los Angeles to New York in a move that seemed more suited to chess than football.

The truth? The Big Ten had been playing a different game all along.

While the Pac-12, ACC, and Big Ten had paraded their alliance in the spotlight, the Big Ten had been strategizing in the shadows. Sun Tzu's words echo here with a bone-chilling clarity: "We cannot enter into alliances until we are acquainted with the designs of our neighbors."

WHERE DID OUR GAME GO?

The Big Ten knew exactly what it wanted. USC and UCLA were pieces in a much larger puzzle, and the Pac-12 never saw the trap being set. The timing of the move wasn't just strategic—it was surgical. The value of the Pac-12 took a massive hit from this one swift strike. They no longer control the second-largest media market in America. Right as they were entering the window for negotiating their next conference media rights deal.

Remember when we said that the deadly scope of the media networks had shifted from the Big 12 to the Pac-12?

Well, Fox now owned the Big Ten AND controlled the second-biggest market in America. Alongside the SEC, the Big Ten cemented itself as a real power conference, stretching its influence coast to coast.

What the strategic alliance was meant to preserve had been shattered in an instant. USC and UCLA's departure from the Pac-12 in 2022 was much like Texas and Oklahoma bolting for the SEC in 2021. This was more than a new conference alignment; rather, it was a warning shot to every school, conference, and player in this evolving battlefield.

There is no loyalty, no tradition, and no alliance that is sacred when power and money are at stake.

And just like that, the Pac-12 had been stripped of its most valuable assets.

The SEC had already won one game, and now the Big Ten was pulling ahead in another.

The alliance? Gone.

Once again, Sun Tzu warned of this. In fact, it could have all been prevented if George Kliavkoff had read up on how commissioners ran leagues. Or if the presidents of Pac-12 schools had selected a commissioner with a history of dealing with college conference politics, or if Kliavkoff had known how to retain his own teams.

A Big Ten insider told us, referring to Pac-12 schools, "Maybe next time, those schools will pick someone smart enough to craft a contract and expect greed from leagues he's been competing against for the last century."

If only someone had read him how Sun Tzu felt about alliances: "We cannot enter into alliances until we are acquainted with the designs of our neighbors."

CHAPTER 12

Being the CEO or executive manager of any organization is like playing 3D chess. As a leader, you are expected to develop a strategy, build consensus around that strategy, and move forward. Invariably, issues and crises develop. Crisis management is in the job description, irrespective of the industry.

You're expected to be the steady hand, the one who navigates the storm when everyone else is losing their minds. And George Kliavkoff had been hired to do just that—lead the Pac-12 back to prominence and guide it through the modern wilderness of college football realignment. His strategy was to negotiate a new media rights deal, which made sense since that is the cornerstone of a conference's existence. However, when crisis erupted, it wasn't just his leadership that was being tested.

The conference's future and his reputation were on the line. The outcome would define his tenure—whether it was good, bad, or ugly.

The key role of the CEO or commissioner is to discern which crises are major and how to address them. You may not realize the extent of the crisis initially, but it is critical to address it relatively quickly. Unfortunately for George Kliavkoff, July 2022 presented him with a very significant crisis. One that was truly multi-faceted.

- Two very prominent schools were leaving the Pac-12.
- The Pac-12 was in the final stages of a media rights deal and had just lost its largest media market—Los Angeles.
- The strategic alliance that was intended to thwart the SEC's dominance had been rendered useless.
- Conferences were fending for themselves, and the Big 12 had just scooped up potential schools that were in contention for Pac-12 expansion.

So, where exactly was George Kliavkoff when the two LA schools left the Pac-12?

Well, interestingly enough, he was on the second day of his vacation in Montana with very limited cell coverage. Kliavkoff likely received a hundred messages from his deputy commissioner, and probably thousands more from others. He returned to Las Vegas promptly and sequestered himself to address these crises.

At this point, the pressure was on George Kliavkoff to recruit high-caliber West Coast teams to replace the two LA schools. But instead, he continued to pursue his strategy of getting a lucrative media rights deal without the second-largest market in the U.S.

Sometimes the crisis is so great that you need to adjust the strategy. Once again, Kliavkoff failed to adjust his strategy, which was a critical catalyst for the demise of the Pac-12.

The second crisis was the media rights deal. Without the two LA teams and with no plans to expand the Pac-12, ESPN came back with a media rights plan. While the amount was consistent with other Power Five schools, it would be much less than their Big Ten and SEC counterparts. Kliavkoff got wind of this and supported the deal... initially.

The value of media rights is only what someone is willing to pay for them. The valuation was relatively weak due to a lack of expansion, but hey. An offer that comes across the table is an offer worth considering.

The third crisis was the abrogation of the strategic alliance less than a year after it had been consummated. In retrospect, the Big Ten did not intend for the alliance to be anything. They used it as their placeholder to address the moves made by the SEC.

Whether the Pac-12 and its member schools were naïve is an open question. Had they looked to philosophers like Sun Tzu or Machiavelli, they might have anticipated the actions that followed. The crisis that landed on Kliavkoff's desk on June 30 was more than just a blow to the Pac-12's media rights negotiations—it was an existential threat. He had to hold the conference together, but time was running out. His vision of the Pac-12 being a mid-tier Power Five conference was becoming less of a vision and more of a pipe dream.

In retrospect, what should have happened is clear. The second the LA schools announced their departure, Kliavkoff should have aggressively pursued expansion—recruiting high-profile west coast teams or aligning the Pac-12 with the Big 12 or even the ACC (with a deal *in writing*). Instead, he stayed the course and pursued a media deal with no future. And with every day that passed without new additions to the conference, its value dropped even further.

In the fallout, Kliavkoff did what he could—but not all he could. He retreated. Away from the press, away from the scrutiny, away from the action. He believed in the media rights deal he was negotiating, even as the cracks in its foundation grew wider. In a telling interview with John Canzano, Kliavkoff admitted to intentionally going silent in the wake of the bombshell news. "I could have spent all day, every day on the phone refuting media reports," he said, "but what I needed to do was get to work."[1] Finally, the commissioner gave a glimpse into his mindset. One that was calculated…but defensive.

Still, as Kliavkoff's early tenure continued on, the conference grew restless. With every passing day, schools like Oregon and Washington began to consider their own futures. Could they survive in a diminished Pac-12, one without USC and UCLA? Could they land a compelling media deal that would allow the conference to compete with the SEC or Big Ten? Or would they, too, be lured by the promise of greener pastures? When Kliavkoff finally stepped into the spotlight again, it was with "uncertain confidence."

First off, Kliavkoff publicly asserted that the Pac-12's media deal would land "in the middle" of the Power Five conferences. He even

---

1. George Kliavkoff, quoted in John Canzano, "Canzano: Pac-12 Commissioner George Kliavkoff Talks Media Rights, Expansion, and More," *JohnCanzano.com*, July 29, 2022, https://www.johncanzano.com/p/canzano-pac-12-commissioner-george.

floated the possibility that teams who reached the playoffs might command a larger share of the financial benefits. By then, however, it was hard to look past the idea that the window might have already closed. The opportunity to salvage the Pac-12 as a major force in college football might have already passed.

Kliavkoff's mistake wasn't just with the media deal or in his handling of USC and UCLA's departure—it was in his failure to pivot when the crisis demanded it. The loss of the Los Angeles market should have triggered a complete reevaluation of the Pac-12's strategy. Instead, Kliavkoff proved unwilling or unable to shift gears in time. Now with the media deal looking like a mere consolation prize, the conference's stability hung by a thread.

One question loomed larger than ever: What could the Pac-12 accept for a media rights deal?

CHAPTER 13

When Larry Scott took over the reins of the Pac-12 from Tom Hansen, the conference was thriving, riding the momentum of years of success. Scott's background as CEO of the Women's Tennis Association (WTA) set him apart from traditional college football figures. Early on though, his tenure quickly proved that experience in media negotiations was more valuable than a football pedigree. At the WTA, Scott expanded the sport into fifty-four countries, landing global broadcasting agreements.

When Scott entered as commissioner of the Pac-12, he united two media powerhouses to orchestrate the largest media rights deal in college sports history. A $3 billion, 12-year contract with Fox and ESPN. This transformative agreement elevated the Pac-12 to the top of the revenue charts, enabling it to surpass every other conference in TV income. Scott also leveraged the opportunity to expand the conference, adding Utah and Colorado and securing critical new markets in Salt Lake City (No.30) and Denver (No.17), respectively.

Under his aggressive leadership, the Pac-12 excelled as the Conference of Champions, and with the run in the late 2000s, the conference seemed poised to dominate for years to come.

A decade later, the Pac-12 would find itself in a far different situation than many had contemplated. George Kliavkoff, hired in 2021 to replace Scott after a decade of his leadership, was brought in with the hope of stabilizing a conference. The Pac-12 was marred by poor performance on the field, and the COVID-19 pandemic left a brutal financial strain. Unlike Scott, Kliavkoff had no background in sports administration. His experience as an MGM Resorts executive was seen as an asset for bringing unity and collaboration. Scott took a more controversial, hard-charging approach. However, what the Pac-12 needed in the decade following Scott was in fact... a fighter. Kliavkoff made it clear he was concerned with being the "nice guy".

Both Scott and Kliavkoff had golden opportunities to capitalize on the University of Texas, as it was one of the most coveted programs in college football. In 2011, Scott had the chance to bring Texas into the Pac-12 as part of a larger expansion effort, but the Longhorns refused to give up the lucrative Longhorn Network they had launched. Unwilling to fold the network into the Pac-12's media structure, Texas stayed with the Big 12... until the SEC came calling.

Where did Texas stand on the Longhorn Network a decade later? This time around, they made it clear they were willing to integrate the Longhorn Network into the larger conference structure of the SEC. The allure of the SEC's broader market eclipsed the benefits that the Longhorn Network could offer. Sure enough, June 30, 2024, was the final broadcast of the Longhorn Network.

The next day, Texas was officially admitted as a member of the SEC.

But where Larry Scott excelled was with Fox and ESPN. These two are rivals, as we've seen, and they came together for the sake of the conference's future. The Pac-12's media rights deal in 2011 became a benchmark for other conferences to follow. It wasn't long before Brett Yormark, the current Big 12 commissioner, used the same strategy to revitalize his own conference. Yormark's 2022 media rights deal is valued at $2.28 billion over six years and stabilized the Big 12. Yormark inked this deal after the retirement of Bob Bowlsby, who was instrumental in expanding the conference, as we have discussed. Yormark studied his predecessor closely and understood the complex landscape of media and conference politics. He avoided the mistakes Kliavkoff made, ensuring Fox and ESPN remained partners without dragging out negotiations over every dime.

Evidently, Kliavkoff miscalculated from the start. Even after the illogical approach of trying to land a media rights deal **before** bolstering the value of his conference, ESPN was willing to bail him out and accept his depleted conference. The network offered $30 million per year for each of the ten remaining Pac-12 schools. Anyone in their right mind accepts that deal and moves forward.

So what did the fervent leader of the faltering Pac-12 conference do? Somehow he was convinced by his board that the conference was worth much more. John Canzano, one of the best in the business, broke down the conversation after Kliavkoff had been led to believe that his conference, suffering massive departures, was due for a huge raise.

"You know what we told ESPN after the $30 million-per-school offer?" said Kliavkoff.

"What?" asked Canzano.

"We said we want $50 million per school."

"And what was the ESPN response?"

"Goodbye."[1]

Another ship had sailed, and another domino had fallen as the Pac-12 inched toward extinction as a Power Five conference. This proved to be a devastating error. Fox, already circling the Pac-12 like a predator, was actively looking to pick off more teams. Kliavkoff's inability to act aggressively (or act…period) made the conference more vulnerable. The loss of USC and UCLA shattered the Pac-12's standing, and Kliavkoff was now scrambling to piece together a media deal. His lack of experience in high-stakes negotiations placed the glorious Pac-12 conference on a slippery slope.

While Scott's tenure had its controversies, his aggressive tactics from an expansion and media negotiations standpoint could have really helped the conference during this time. At this point, Kliavkoff's reputation was battered with missed opportunities and missteps. Whether Scott would have fought to retain the conference's top programs or simply cut his losses and taken whatever deal was given, ultimately, we will never know. One thing is for certain: it would have been better than Kliavkoff's slow approach, which turned lackadaisical past a certain point.

---

1. Kliavkoff, "Pac-12 Commissioner George Kliavkoff Talks Media Rights."

At this point, the conference faced an uncertain future. Rich history and tradition hung in the balance. The Pac-12, home to historic rivalries, Rose Bowl triumphs, and decades of perennial athletic excellence, now sat on the edge of oblivion. What had once been a proud cornerstone of college sports was in danger of being wiped away entirely. Its storied legacy was at risk of fading into the background as other conferences grew stronger. Would the Pac-12 survive, or would its proud history become a mere footnote in the ever-evolving landscape of collegiate athletics?

The future was uncertain, and the next moves would determine whether the Pac-12 would rise once again or be forever lost to the pages of history. The story wasn't over, but as time ran out, one question lingered—would the Conference of Champions endure, or had its final chapter already been written?

CHAPTER 14

Larry Scott's tenure as Pac-12 commissioner is a story worth learning from. Scott answered <u>not</u> to the athletic directors who ran the day-to-day operations of their schools' sports programs, but instead to the university chancellors. Although the conference was clearly one of the best in the country, this style of leadership restricts input from the athletically driven people. So how might that affect an athletic conference?

This was a key flaw in the governance structure that would continuously haunt the Pac-12 under Scott's leadership, which was defined by ambition, ego, and missed opportunities. The university chancellors were not appointed as sports administrators. They weren't hired to be concerned with having a successful athletic conference. These were full-bred academic leaders.

Every athletic department in the country (that has a football program) relies on the revenue from football to subsidize every other sport. In some instances, there is basketball, which barely pays for itself. Despite this, Scott focused on appeasing the chancellors of the schools, who had little interest in making sports the priority it needed to be.

The truth is, West Coast schools never had quite the same passion for sports as their counterparts in the Big Ten or the SEC. For many Pac-12 universities, football—and athletics in general—was not central to the institutions' missions. Academics came first, and sports, while respected, were not the core of the universities' identities. Unlike powerhouse programs in the Southeast and Midwest, Pac-12 programs lacked the institutional drive to make athletics a priority. The chancellors were naturally more interested in research budgets than in football revenue, creating a unique challenge for Scott. He needed to be savvy enough to rally these uninterested representatives of their athletics programs around a unified vision. He proved to be unwilling, or simply unable, to do so.

Viewership suffered throughout Scott's tenure, and the Pac-12's ratings nosedived. What initially seemed like a harmless scheduling quirk turned into a revenue drain, as fans—even diehards—simply stopped tuning in.

Initially, Scott's media rights deal appeared to be an innovative approach to alter the sports media landscape. As time went on, however, cracks in the foundation began to show. By the middle of his tenure, the conference's performance began a steady decline. This poor performance from around the conference, coupled with games being scheduled at odd, late-night hours, didn't prove to be very profitable.

WHERE DID OUR GAME GO?

In an effort to take advantage of a time slot with no competition from other power conferences, Scott established "Pac-12 After Dark." While these games provided many upsets and high-scoring West Coast football, they ultimately became the punchline to a cruel joke. "After dark" typically meant a kickoff at 10 p.m. ET or later. Remember, the East Coast fans have their favorite teams kick off as early as noon ET. There was no interest from these people, almost 12 hours of football later, to tune into a game a thousand miles away.

The SEC and Big Ten thrived on consistent prime-time slots, commanding huge audiences across the country. The 3:30 p.m. ET and 7 p.m. ET kickoff slots were perfect for marquee matchups across the country; a game at these times was shown at lunchtime on the West Coast or in the late afternoon. I know; it's unfair. But hey, try kicking off earlier in the morning, at the same times as other conferences. At least the door would be open for fans across the country to tune in.

The Pac-12's late-night games seemed to be appreciated only by serious diehards, further hurting the brand and causing serious drops in revenue. Advertisers weren't willing to pay top dollar for games no one was watching, and TV networks began to lose interest. The pendulum was swinging back on the Pac-12's rise as well. By 2018, the battered and bruised Pac-12, with some of the worst TV ratings in the country, stumbled to a 1–8 record in bowl games and went winless in March Madness. Slowly but surely, the Pac-12 was becoming irrelevant in the national conversation, and Scott seemed either oblivious or indifferent to the problem.

One of the most controversial aspects of Scott's reign was the creation of the Pac-12 Network. In theory, it was a brilliant idea—a network entirely owned by the conference, offering 24/7 coverage of Pac-12 sports. It was Scott's pride and joy. Unlike other conferences that partnered with major broadcasters like ESPN or Fox, Scott loved that the Pac-12 retained 100 percent ownership of the network. He rejected offers from cable partners, *multiple times,* that would have boosted the network's reach and revenue, especially as college football aficionados across the country went out late.

Partnering with major networks would have put the conference in a position to be showcased at restaurants, bars, etc., across the country. Scott, presented with this incredible opportunity... decided to pass on introducing the rest of the country to the Pac-12, at times making it easier for Seattle residents to watch Florida and Alabama play instead of Washington and Oregon State.

The long-term result? While the SEC and Big Ten Network flourished with wide distribution and lucrative contracts, the Pac-12 Network floundered. Consistently available in only a fraction of the households that other conference networks reached, it never generated the kind of revenue necessary to compete at the highest level.

Scott's decision to hold on to ownership at the expense of distribution was perhaps his greatest misstep. The network never took off in the way he imagined, and its limited reach became a symbol of the conference's broader problems. After several years, the Big Ten Network brought in an estimated 68 million subscribers, and the SEC sat comfortably at 57 million. How did the Pac-12 Network do? Well, they put up a pathetic 11 million in ratings. Instead of focusing on expanding the Pac-12's footprint and fan base, Scott was more interested in controlling the narrative, even if it meant stifling the very growth the conference so desperately needed.

Adding to the frustration was Scott's apparent disinterest in the actual games. Stories of him leaving football games early to return to his office in downtown San Francisco only added to the perception that he, along with the school's chancellors, didn't really care about athletics. For someone tasked with leading one of the nation's most prominent collegiate conferences, Scott often seemed more concerned with the optics of his leadership—managing the chancellors, hosting meetings in the Pac-12's luxurious San Francisco headquarters, and preserving the conference's image. He appeared to be concerned far less with the sustained health and success of the sports themselves.

The move to relocate the Pac-12 headquarters from Walnut Creek to San Francisco's Financial District was another glaring example of Scott's detachment from reality. He invested nearly $100 million over 12 years to lease office space in one of the most expensive real estate markets in the world. A state-of-the-art television studio was built into the headquarters, and the facility was designed to impress—though few seemed to understand why the conference needed such an extravagant home. The member schools, many of them public institutions facing budget cuts, footed the bill. Meanwhile, the question hung in the air: *Who exactly was visiting this lavish headquarters, and why did the Pac-12 need it?* For Scott, it seemed more about prestige than practicality.

Scott ignored the athletic directors, who could have guided him through the complexities of running a sports conference. Instead, he fixated on making the chancellors happy despite their lack of engagement with athletics. He also found a way to take the hottest conference in the country, home of the flashy Oregon Ducks, the storied Southern California Trojans, and the dominant Washington Huskies, and steer them toward irrelevance, failing to adapt as other conferences surged ahead in revenue, exposure, and national prominence.

The late-night games, the botched network, and the obnoxious San Francisco headquarters were the enduring symbols of a conference that had lost its way—and a commissioner who never seemed to understand what really mattered.

Larry Scott's tenure at the helm of the Pac-12 was already teetering when COVID-19 hit. This global pandemic became the final chapter of a saga that had seen moments of brilliance drowned out by a deluge of poor decisions and unchecked ego. By then, Scott had already driven the conference to the brink. Revenues were plummeting, the Pac-12 Network was an unmitigated disaster, and the infamous "Pac-12 After Dark" broadcasts were alienating fans. Then came COVID, changing everything.

The COVID-19 pandemic swept across the world, shuttering businesses, closing schools, and throwing sports into chaos. Conference commissioners faced unprecedented decisions.

None faltered quite like Larry Scott. His response?

Furlough 94 of the Pac-12's 196 employees—a staggering half of the workforce. Those who had worked tirelessly to prop up the conference were left in the cold while Scott, stunningly, took a massive bonus. At a time when leadership demanded sacrifice and solidarity, Scott's priorities were as clear as ever—himself. His decisions weren't just a reflection of poor management; they were a direct insult to those struggling to keep the lights on at their respective universities and within the Pac-12 offices.

But most damning of all was Scott's handling of the Pac-12 football season. While the SEC, Big Ten, and others were developing plans for limited schedules, safety protocols, and ways to keep the revenue machine running, Scott's knee-jerk reaction was to cancel the football season entirely. No consultation with players. No conversations with coaches. No outreach to the athletic directors whose very livelihoods depended on a functioning football program. The Pac-12, under Scott's leadership, simply folded.

What Scott didn't expect was the tidal wave of backlash from the very people he had ignored for so long: players pushed back. Coaches made their frustrations known. Even the broader college football world criticized his decision. For perhaps the first time in his tenure, Scott felt the weight of public opinion bearing down on him. Under pressure, he relented—but it was too late. A truncated season was slapped together with no fans and four scheduled games per team. Some teams did not play certain games due to COVID-19 restrictions.

What should have been a lifeline for the conference was a hollow, last-ditch effort to save face.

Yet again, Scott had misjudged the role sports play in society. When the world is in crisis, sports often become a refuge, a source of hope and unity. Throughout history, major world events have rattled the foundation of athletics. Whether it was World War II shutting down entire leagues or the banning of sports during times of unrest in the early 1900s, COVID certainly did the same.

The pandemic revealed the truth about Larry Scott's tenure: when the league needed his leadership, Scott faltered. COVID became the crown jewel of his misguided reign, seeping into the cracks that had been growing for years.

In the end, it wasn't just the mismanagement of a football season or the botched TV deal. When major world events hit, sports are profoundly affected. More importantly, history has shown what sports should do during divisive times. Scott goes down as the leader who failed to lead, and the pandemic was the nail in the coffin.

CHAPTER 15

As the college football world rounded the corner from COVID, it was poised for a new opportunity. For the Pac-12, Larry Scott's tumultuous reign had finally ended. A fresh start beckoned, and the conference seemed ready to reclaim its place at the pinnacle of collegiate athletics. When Larry Scott walked out of the Pac-12's San Francisco office for the last time, it was the end of an era—a messy, extravagant, head-scratching era.

He left behind a conference bruised from a decade of questionable decisions, but it was still breathing and sat hopeful. This conference has survived world wars; certainly it can survive a rough patch, right?

Enter George Kliavkoff, a man who believed in clean slates and fresh starts. That hope hummed loudly, capturing the attention of fans and media across the landscape. Recruits flocked from all across the country as new opportunities beckoned out west. However, this hope and excitement quickly dimmed as reality breached the surface. You reap what you sow in life, and the same is true for college athletic conferences.

Only a year and a half later, ESPN walked away from media rights negotiations, and Fox, once a partner, circled like a hungry vulture, eager to pick off what remained of the conference. George Kliavkoff found himself at the helm of a ship headed straight for an iceberg.

As we highlighted before, Kliavkoff also turned down multiple expansion opportunities, insisting that the conference could secure a deal that would keep them competitive.

Fans were confused. Teams were restless. Employees, once assured by Kliavkoff's calm demeanor, were beginning to wonder if they were standing on the deck of that sinking ship. The Pac-12's once-bright future under a new commissioner was fading fast. However, Kliavkoff remained convinced that everything was under control. In his mind, there was no reason to worry.

When it came time for Kliavkoff to reveal his master plans, they were... underwhelming. Perhaps a bit disastrous? You be the judge.

To start, he believed he could block UCLA's departure to the Big Ten and keep them in the fold by lobbying the Board of Regents to prevent the move. The cost? Fifty-two million dollars. Kliavkoff expressed interest in paying this, as UCLA's departure looked to punch a massive hole in the conference. Oregon, who had been committed to the Pac-12 through 2022 and into 2023, made its position clear: if UCLA made more money, Oregon wouldn't be sticking around.

And just like that, the move was finalized. Ten teams remaining. No media rights deal.

Then, from out of nowhere, Kliavkoff had what he thought was his moment of brilliance. His salvation. He realized that retaining Oregon was the key. The Ducks, one of the most iconic brands in college football, were backed by Nike billionaire Phil Knight. This was Kliavkoff's last hope. So he went to work, scrambling to craft a streaming deal with Apple—a modern solution for a modern problem. Most importantly, Phil Knight was all in. If there was any chance of saving the Pac-12, this was it.

By the time August 2023 rolled around, the Pac-12 was no longer just negotiating from a place of weakness—it was on the verge of extinction. All the pieces that had been set in motion over the past year seemed ready to collide. Think about everything this conference had been through. The failed mergers. The strategic alliance. The botched media rights negotiations. Rejected expansion opportunities. The seismic loss of UCLA and USC. A full decade of poor management.

The twilight zone that the Pac-12 had been trapped in suddenly became its reality.

Would the Apple deal save the Pac-12 at the 11th hour? Could Kliavkoff's last-ditch effort pull the conference back from the brink? Or was it all just too little, too late? For a brief, surreal moment, everything seemed possible.

Thinking back to this day, it felt like anything could happen. Someone said the circumstances here brought them back to a rare moment in college football history when there was a lot in flux. Everything actually *was* on the table.

Just about anything that *could* happen...did.

CHAPTER 16

In the long history of college football, there have been moments that have transcended the game, where the very soul of the sport was on the line, and everything was on the table.

Perhaps the perfect example of this is from a school you've never heard of.

In the fall of 1899, deep in the hills of East Tennessee, a team of 18 men gathered on the remote campus of Sewanee. Sewanee sits roughly an hour northwest of Chattanooga and is known as "The University of the South." They were dominant back in the day and even helped charter the Southeastern Conference. Yes, it was the same SEC you watch today: charter member Sewanee Tigers.

These men weren't football stars in the modern sense—there were no scholarships, no national spotlights, no grand stadiums filled with tens of thousands of fans. As proud alumni and Sewanee football aficionado Norman Jetmundsen put it, "These boys were just students who loved the game. They didn't know they were about to make history."[1]

Sewanee was a tiny, isolated school. In this era, however, it was home to the "Iron Men" who accomplished one of the wildest feats in sports history.

With only 18 players, they embarked on a 2,500-mile journey across the South, playing five games in six days. It began in Austin, Texas, where the Tigers faced off against the University of Texas. At the time,

---

1. Norman Jetmundsen, quoted in Meredith Garrett, "Bringing the Iron Men to Life," *The University of the South*, accessed 2024, https://new.sewanee.edu/features/bringing-the-iron-men-to-life/.

WHERE DID OUR GAME GO?

Texas was already a burgeoning powerhouse, but Sewanee walked away with a 12–0 victory.

That was just the beginning.

From Austin, the team rolled into Houston, where they played Texas A&M and won 10–0. With barely a breath, they boarded the train again, heading to New Orleans to take on Tulane, dispatching them 23–0. Next was Baton Rouge, where they crushed LSU 34–0, and finally, in Memphis, they finished their brutal trip by shutting out Ole Miss 12–0.

In six days, playing five games against five of the toughest teams in the region, the Sewanee Tigers had done the impossible. They hadn't just won—they went through it all without giving up a single point.

This team has gone down as one of the greatest in college football history, next to the 2001 Miami Hurricanes, 1995 Nebraska Cornhuskers, and 2019 LSU Tigers. It was a moment when anything seemed possible, when the impossible became reality. The Iron Men embodied the sport's raw, unfiltered power.

Fast forward more than a century, and the west coast equivalent conference, founded in the same era as the 1899 Sewanee Tigers, was facing its own reckoning—only this time, it wasn't triumph that awaited.

On August 4, 2023, everything was on the table—not in the foothills of Appalachia but all along the West Coast. Instead of glory, the conference that had long been woven into the fabric of college football was about to unravel before everyone's eyes.

For someone like Yogi Roth, who had lived and breathed Pac-12 football for years, the collapse of the conference felt like a slow-motion disaster. One moment, the future seemed secure—a deal with Apple was nearly signed, optimism was high, and there was hope that the conference could survive. The next, it all fell apart.

Roth had spent the night before in Venice Beach, sitting with Marcus Arroyo at Scopa, discussing the uncertain future of the conference. Like the Sewanee Iron Men staring down impossible odds and emerging victorious, Roth hoped that something could be salvaged—that somehow, the Pac-12 would endure. But deep down, as he watched the LA Rams practice, he knew the odds weren't in their favor. Within hours, his worst fears were confirmed.

Oregon and Washington announced a move to the Big Ten, setting off a chain reaction that would decimate the Pac-12.

The exodus had begun.

Utah, Arizona, and Arizona State left for the Big 12 later that day, along with Colorado who had announced earlier.

Soon after, UC Berkeley and Stanford soon joined the ACC.

Just like that.

It didn't take but a few days.

Over a century of tradition, rivalries, and history had been wiped away.

And there the Pac-12 sat.

A hollow shell of what it once was.

For Roth, it felt like being on a rollercoaster: at the peak one moment and plummeting the next. Everything he and his colleagues had worked for over the past decade.

Every broadcast.

Every game.

It was all now up in the air.

What made it worse was the disbelief.

Just the day before, Roth had clung to the possibility of salvation.

Surely, the Pac-12 could weather this storm. After all, it had survived for over a hundred years, shaping the identity of West Coast football. Hosting several national championship squads, thousands of professional players, and iconic moments. Not just relevant in college football history but in sports history.

As the Iron Men turned impossible odds into victory, the Pac-12 floundered in the dog days before the 2023 football season. Everything crumbled in front of their eyes.

The fans were left stunned.

The teams, players, and coaches who had once called the Pac-12 home were off to greener pastures. The two remaining teams, Washington State and Oregon State, hung in the balance, along with over a century's worth of history.

CHAPTER 17

And so here we are, at the beginning of the next chapter of the American phenomenon that is college football. Sitting without a legendary conference that stretched across the Cascades and the Rockies and captured the imaginations of millions. Mismanagement, ego, and short-sighted decisions defined the final era of Pac-12 football. It was a recipe for disaster—and a disaster it was.

The end of the Pac-12 as we knew it was not a sudden, tragic collapse but rather a slow bleed caused by a series of missed opportunities and consecutive bad gambles from poor leaders.

By the summer of 2024, Washington State and Oregon State stood alone in a desolate landscape. Their conference peers were off to richer pastures in the Big Ten, Big 12, and ACC. The conference arms race that rose out of media greed had come down to these three, while the SEC sat on its throne and watched.

That's what college football has become.

The great debate stands: Is this for better or for worse? Players are finally getting a cut of the millions of dollars they generate for their universities; many would argue that it is long overdue. The athlete's name, image, and likeness landscape has been publicly established. Players can now monetize their image thanks to years of litigation, many opting to hire agents to have a professional help navigate the landscape. However, some feel that we've lost the essence of what makes our game so great.

The first issue people point to is a lack of loyalty. Players no longer commit to one program for a college tenure. The transfer portal has made it such that players can move back and forth, some playing for a different team every year. Yes, every year.

Events like National Signing Day, where high school athletes across the country execute their letters of intent for a four-year institution, are rendered unimportant.

New conference realignments have made for better matchups throughout the season. However, that came at the expense of discarding a century of rich history and tradition. What remained of the Pac-12 by the fall of 2024 was the "Pac-2," a sad shell of abandoned teams in poor TV markets that no one was willing to swoop in and save.

As Washington stormed through their final season in the Pac-12, going undefeated and playing for the national title, the irony was palpable—**the best season in Pac-12 football history** unfolded as the conference (and the game, as we knew it) was taking its dying breaths.

Just to give you a brief rundown of how the Pac-12 conference made history in its final year:

- Washington quarterback Michael Penix Jr. led the nation with 4,903 passing yards.
- Oregon's Bo Nix was second with 4,508 passing yards.
    - No other QB in the country had 4,000 passing yards outside of these two.
    - Two of the top three Heisman finalists were Pac-12 players, with USC QB Caleb Williams winning the prior year and being selected as the number one pick of the NFL Draft following the 2023 season.
    - Three of the top six players in receiving yards were Pac-12 players.
    - Rome Odunze from UW led the nation in receiving yards with 1,640.
    - The conference went 89–66 overall, with a 57.4% win percentage, the second-highest among all conferences.
        - The conference's strength of schedule was number one in the NCAA.
    - The week three poll (September 23, 2023) had eight of the 12 Pac-12 teams ranked.
        - Much of this was due to the Pac-12's very strong non-conference showing.
- The Pac-12 was one of only two conferences with a winning record (62.5% win rate) against the other four power conferences.
- The Big 12 was the only other conference to achieve this, with a 52.6% win rate against other power conferences.

- Year of the QB:
    - The Pac-12 had three QBs drafted in the top 12 of the NFL draft, with every one of those QBs having finished in the top three of the Heisman voting at some point during their collegiate careers.
- The Pac-12 had the second-most NFL draft picks in 2024, and the conference ahead of it, the SEC, had two more conference members.
- The National Football Foundation's Campbell Trophy was awarded to Oregon QB Bo Nix.
- The Pac-12 championship game was a showdown between the Washington Huskies and the Oregon Ducks, a playoff-clinching event that was the most-viewed conference championship game in history. The Huskies walked away victorious and proceeded to take down the Texas Longhorns in the CFP Semifinal, earning a berth in the national championship game.

Even a team like Oregon State rode heavy as a scrappy two-loss team, ranked No.11 in the final weeks of the season and pushing the undefeated Washington Huskies to the brink in a 22–20 loss. As glorious as the Pac-12 run in 2023 was, the season had an eerie feel to it—we all collectively knew this would be the last time we cheered for a champion under the banner of the Pac-12, a feat rarely seen across sports.

The writing had been on the wall long before the final whistle, both for the game and for the conference. Players were starting to don multiple uniforms over their four-year careers. NIL collectives were formed to construct deals that lured players to their program, often times with heavy compensation. As for the Pac-12, the commissioner who had promised to make the Pac-12 a media giant had grossly misunderstood the nature of college athletics. Larry Scott's tenure was filled with grand ideas but poor execution. By the time George Kliavkoff took over in 2021, the damage was pretty bad. Kliavkoff's task was to save the conference. To pull it back from the brink of irrelevance and negotiate a media rights deal.

Instead, he was the second problematic hire and only accelerated the decline. But, he did piece together a media rights deal that united all parties... to leave the conference rather than stay.

At the 2023 Pac-12 Media Day, Kliavkoff sat before a room of reporters, smiling, as if the ship wasn't already halfway sunk. His answers were a masterclass in evasion.

"We constantly update our board. I think they're enthusiastic, like I am, about the media deal. I will tell you what we've seen is that the longer we wait for the media deal, the better our options get. I think our board realizes that."

His next comments were the peak of his ignorance.

"Our schools are committed to each other and the Pac-12. We'll get our media rights deal done. We'll announce the deal. I think the realignment that's going on in college athletics will come to an end for this cycle."

It was such a weak performance on-stage that Colorado, whose head football coach was not present for media day, announced their departure for the Big 12 conference a few days later.

Ultimately, this conference fell because of the very thing that makes college football great—competition. This time, however, the competition wasn't on the field; it was behind closed doors. For a while, it seemed like this might be the end of West Coast football as we knew it.

But sport, like life, finds a way to continue and thrive.

Washington State and Oregon State, the last two soldiers standing, were determined to keep the league alive. During the interim period, they worked with the Mountain West to put together a schedule for 2024, and there were whispers of something more permanent on the horizon.

The question everyone had been asking finally had an answer—who in the world could step into the role of commissioner and save what little was left of a two-team conference in Pullman, WA (66th media market) and Corvallis, OR (120th)? Enter Theresa Gould, a longtime **college sports** administrator.

Alas, the Pac-12 had appointed someone with the right kind of experience, the first since Tom Hansen in 1983. Gould brought deep ties to the Mountain West Conference. She is not the brash, media-obsessed figure her predecessors were. Instead, as Washington State University President and chair of the Pac-12 Board of Directors Kirk Schulz put it, she held "a deep knowledge of collegiate athletics and unwavering commitment to student-athletes." This alongside a resumé of success "makes her uniquely qualified to help guide the Pac-12 Conference during this period of unprecedented change in college sports."[1]

---

1. Kirk Schulz, quoted in "Pac-12 Appoints Teresa Gould as Commissioner to Lead Future Success of Conference," *Pac-12 Conference*, February 19, 2024, https://pac-12.com/article/2024/02/19/pac-12-appoints-teresa-gould-commissioner-lead-future-success-conference.

Schulz wouldnt stop singing Theresa Gould's praises. "As the first female commissioner of an Autonomy Five conference,[2] Teresa will be able to bring new perspectives and fresh ideas to the table as the industry works to find its way through this shifting landscape.

We look forward to her leadership as we write the next chapter in the Pac-12's storied history."

Gould, in her first statement as commissioner, said the following:

"I look forward to partnering with Oregon State and Washington State to secure a bright future for their student-athletes that allows them to compete at the highest level of college athletics while enjoying the benefits of a quality campus experience. Working in collaboration with their leadership and our talented staff, I am excited to build a pathway for the future that allows their programs to thrive."

Could she be the one to spearhead the Pac-12 into a prosperous new era? Time will tell. Her leadership so far has been nothing short of remarkable. "For over a century, the Pac-12 Conference has been recognized as a leading brand in intercollegiate athletics," Gould added, "We will continue to pursue bold, cutting-edge opportunities for growth and progress to best serve our member institutions and student-athletes… An exciting new era for the Pac-12 Conference begins today."

This was said in the fall of 2024 at the announcement of four schools, Colorado State, Fresno State, Boise State, and San Diego State, who will join the conference as full members in the summer of 2026.

---

2. The Pac-12 is not officially listed as A5, as the NCAA or whoever has modified the use and made it A4.

Washington State and Oregon State maintained membership status, and the conference continued to make calls.

Over the next several months, Utah State, Boise State, and Texas State all announced their membership as well. These eight teams not only kept the Pac-12 alive, but also competed in the FBS.

The league has made it clear that it is here to stay; membership expanded to top media markets and high-performing programs. The Pac-12 conference will surely look different, but kudos to Theresa Gould. Under her leadership, the conference will survive and compete in the Football Bowl Subdivision.

Now, in and amongst the fire emerges a new era. For the entity that is the Pac-12, they finally have a calculated plan aimed at embracing a future that preserves the rich traditions of West Coast football. For the first time in years, the conference has ambition again. Theresa Gould has given the conference a pulse, but whether it regains its stature as a national powerhouse remains to be seen. Expansion could bring new life—or further dilute what was left of its legacy.

The chaos, uncertainty, and heartbreak that so many fans felt is finally ceasing. As with all things in sports, an ending only made way for a new beginning. Could this conference one day rise again and pull in powerhouse programs to restore its place in the national conversation?

The drama isn't over.

So we've seen the direction the game is going, but what lies ahead for the Pac-12's reincarnation? Optimism runs high, but recent history has shown how leadership can make or break even the most promising visions.

The lesson here is clear: no conference is too big to fail, and no tradition is too sacred to fall victim to greed. But maybe, just maybe, this new chapter will be different. Maybe, after everything, the Pac-12 will find its way back to prominence. Again, time will tell. We watch. We wait. And we will adamantly seek to validate whatever rumors spread because, these days, nothing is beyond the realm of possibility in college athletics.

And for those still bitter over the collapse of the original Pac-12, stretching back to the PCC in 1915, remember the 2023 Washington Huskies.

Yes, it was a bittersweet farewell—but what a farewell it was.

The 2023 Huskies were the only team *ever* to go undefeated in the regular season, win the Pac-12 conference championship game, earn a berth in the College Football Playoff, dominate their semifinal, and field a team with the beloved Pac-12 shield on their right shoulder in the national championship game, all in one season. All of it in the final season of the Pac-12 as we knew it.

Though the Huskies knew they would be ending an era as the Pac-12's final major team of prominence, the season would be one to savor for an eternity.

You couldn't write it any better, but we sure tried our best.

CONCLUSION

As we close the curtain on this exploration of college football's billion-dollar transformation, it is clear that the sport stands on the precipice of a new era—one defined by innovation, upheaval, and opportunity. The 2024 season, which introduced the much-anticipated 12-team College Football Playoff, has already begun to reshape the competitive landscape. For years, critics of the four-team format argued it catered to the sport's perennial powerhouses, leaving little room for smaller schools or non-traditional contenders. But this expanded playoff format has altered the narrative, offering new life to programs and fan bases that once viewed a championship berth as an unattainable dream.

Programs like SMU, which finished 8-0 in ACC play during their inaugural season in the conference, serve as the perfect example of this shift. The Mustangs, leveraging a mix of NIL-driven recruiting and transfer portal acquisitions, have shown that emerging programs can now make a legitimate case for national recognition. Similarly, Indiana and Duke, both led by first-year head coaches, showcased dramatic turnarounds that injected fresh energy into their programs and elevated the ACC's overall competitiveness. Where did Arizona State come from? Projected to finish dead last in conference rankings for their inaugural season in the Big 12 conference, they pulled off the impossible, winning the conference and taking Texas to double overtime in the playoff Quarterfinal round. The playoff's inclusivity has given rise to these stories of resilience and resurgence, upholding the longstanding tradition of college football Saturdays being unpredictable, week in and week out.

However, the sport's evolution has brought challenges that will define its future. The NCAA's House settlement regarding name, image, and likeness (NIL) came down in 2025 and represents a seismic shift. The proposal aims to guarantee athletes a piece of the revenue that their performances help generate. For top-tier programs like Georgia, Michigan, and Ohio State, this settlement offers an opportunity to leverage their financial dominance to secure elite talent. Yet, the proposal raises significant concerns; we saw the ramifications that the NIL law had in 2021. This new era risks widening the gap between the haves and have-nots unless conferences and collectives can craft equitable solutions.

One potential innovation comes from the Pac-12. The conference is exploring the idea of a shared NIL fund that pools revenue from marquee matchups and redistributes it to member schools. While critics worry this approach might dilute competitive advantages for top programs, proponents see it as a necessary step to preserve parity in a landscape increasingly defined by financial disparities.

Another cultural shift that reflects the professionalization of college football is the emergence of the general manager role within programs. Once reserved for the NFL, the GM position has become indispensable in navigating the complexities of the transfer portal and NIL negotiations. Programs across the country have hired seasoned professionals to oversee roster construction, turning what was once a recruiting process into a strategic operation akin to managing a pro franchise. These GMs are not merely administrative figures; they are seen more as architects, responsible for building championship-caliber rosters while ensuring compliance with ever-evolving regulations.

Innovation is not limited to personnel strategies. Programs across the nation are continuing to invest heavily in facilities and technology to gain a competitive edge. Perhaps the "technological-athlete arms race" is what's next for our game. As we look ahead, the role of the NCAA remains one of the biggest questions in college football's future. The organization that once governed every aspect of the sport now finds itself increasingly questioned by powerful parties throughout the sport. With the SEC and Big Ten generating billions through their media rights deals, some insiders speculate the NCAA's role could diminish to little more than an administrative facilitator. If this trend continues, the future of college football may be shaped more by corporate interests than by traditional governance.

And yet, amidst this whirlwind of change, the heart of college football —the passion, the traditions, and the sense of community—endures. Irrespective of who takes the field, how these rosters are assembled, or whatever whirlwind millions of fans endured that off-season, early September will roll around. Calendars will start to fill up with plans to trek to our favorite institutions of higher learning, and these universities will prepare for an influx of tens of thousands of fans week after week after week.

As we close this story, we are left with a sport in flux, but one that remains as captivating as ever. College football's future will be defined by how it adapts to the whirlwind of changes that the game is poised to undergo. But through it all, we can rest easy knowing that the essence of the game endures: the roar of the crowd, the pageantry of fall Saturdays, and the unyielding spirit of competition won't be going anywhere.

This is a sport that mirrors the American spirit—innovative, resilient, and passionately embraced by millions. The stage is set for a future as unpredictable and thrilling as the game itself, and for the fans who gather every Saturday, that future will unfold before our very eyes. And if you think you know something, don't bet on it because the shifts in this sport are just getting started.

AFTERWORD
BY NICK DOUGLAS

I couldn't have imagined what I was getting myself into when I approached Dean with the idea for this project.

I was sitting in the remote desert of Abu Dhabi at four in the morning, more than 8,000 miles away from the bustling college football stadiums, just days after seeing Michigan emerge over Washington as national champion. As I came down from the high that was the college football season, my mind raced with thoughts about the sport.

It's a surreal feeling to be so far removed geographically from American football after it's been your heartbeat for the last several months. Yet, there Dean and I were, deep into a discussion about college football. This conversation took up several hours, and we covered the future and what recent developments in the sport might mean to fans, media members, administrators, and athletes. The fact of the matter was that our sport had grown and evolved in ways no one could have predicted.

AFTERWORD

Digesting the national championship, I continued to remark on the sheer magnitude of what this sport means to everyone around it. That's when we decided to work on this project to clarify the situation around college football.

We traveled time and again across the country, from Los Angeles to Seattle, back to LA, and everywhere in between. Soaking in the history and passion has been fascinating, and learning about the monumental games and subtle nuances of conference politics has been a journey that we will never forget.

As we wrap things up, we want to extend our deepest gratitude to everyone who made this story possible, starting with the Benis brothers, Nick and Chris. Your contributions throughout this process have been stellar. We are indebted to you both greatly. Thank you so much.

We'd also like to thank the sports administrators and insiders who provided behind-the-scenes insight and the historians who illuminated the rich traditions of the sport for us. As for the fans, their passion for the sport was electric, reminding us of how college football serves as a unifying force.

Most of you preferred to remain anonymous, but all of you have played an integral role in bringing this book to life. We are grateful for your trust, openness, and willingness to engage in these conversations, which helped bring this complex and evolving tale to the page. You know who you are, and we appreciate you.

Telling the story of college football and the Pac-12—arguably one of the most storied conferences in the sport's history—has been an honor. There is something undeniably special about these places—the stadiums, the communities, and the traditions. The people we met

AFTERWORD

along the way and their pride, memories, and unwavering love for the game are what gave life to this book. As we said in the beginning, this game is not just a sport. It's a way of life.

As we look to the future, we remain excited about what lies ahead. Though the landscape will change, the essence of the game endures. Its heartbeat—its fans, players, and history—will keep it alive through whatever transformations come its way. The solutions that arise for the challenges the sport faces may be unknown. One thing is for certain, however: college football will continue to thrive.

Thank you for being a part of this journey and for sharing your love for a sport that continues to shape so many lives. This has been a privilege, and we can't wait to see what comes next for our sport, for us, and for you.

THANK YOU FOR READING OUR BOOK!

Just to say thanks for buying and reading our book, we'd love to connect!
To Download Now, Visit:

We appreciate your interest in our book and value your feedback as it helps us improve future versions. We would appreciate it if you could leave your invaluable review on Amazon.com with your feedback. Thank you!

www.ingramcontent.com/pod-product-compliance
Lightning Source LLC
Chambersburg PA
CBHW030247010526
44107CB00031B/1353/J